BEARING THE CROSS

BEARING THE CROSS

MY INSPIRING JOURNEY FROM POVERTY TO THE NFL AND SPORTS TELEVISION

IRV CROSS

WITH CLIFTON BROWN

FOREWORD BY GIL BRANDT

SPORTS PUBLISHING

Visit our website at www.sportspubbooks.com.

10 9 8 7 6 5 4 3 2 1

Library of Congress Cataloging-in-Publication Data is available on file.

Cover design by Tom Lau
Cover photographs courtesy of Macalester College and AP Images

Print ISBN: 978-1-68358-117-8
Ebook ISBN: 978-1-68358-118-5

Printed in the United States of America

Irv:
This book is dedicated to an old-fashioned teacher who cared about a poor, lost boy. I was in the fifth grade when my mother passed away and, my teacher, Miss Ruth Ewing, took me from a state of depression to a positive outlook on life. She is the one person who influenced my life more than any other, and this book is written in her memory.

Clifton:
To my three heartbeats: Delores, Ashley, and Alex
And to my three role models: George Brown, Maurita Brown, and Georgia Richardson

AUTHOR'S NOTE

I **HAVE** indeed lived a storied life. In the seventy-eight years that I have been on this planet, I have seen a lot. Unfortunately, the more you see the more difficult it is to remember it all.

In the time I spent with Clifton Brown, we discussed my life for hours. While many of those stories appear in the text you will soon read, there were often times where I could not remember a specific detail or event. Thankfully, Clifton was able to speak with those who were on this journey that is life with me, and helped fill in the blanks. I appreciate them all for taking the time to speak with him and for sharing memories of our time together.

The goal of this book was to share my journey, and I hope you are able to appreciate it as much as I have.

God is good, and enjoy me *Bearing the Cross* for you all.

Irv Cross
May 2017

TABLE OF CONTENTS

FOREWORD BY GIL BRANDT

MY fondest memory of Irv Cross is flying on an airplane with him from Philadelphia (PA) to Columbus (OH) back in the early seventies. That was the rockiest plane ride I've ever had. And that's saying something. I've been on thousands of flights in my life, working for twenty-nine years as the Dallas Cowboys vice president of player personnel, followed by the work I'm doing today for the NFL and NFL.com.

However, this plane trip was particularly brutal. I thought we were going to crash. We would drop 50 feet without warning, and we were getting jostled around like we were tennis balls.

Obviously we didn't crash because then I wouldn't be telling this story. The entire plane ride, Irv never lost his cool. That was my first time witnessing how cool Irv really is under pressure. His calmness during that ride was amazing. I mean, if a flight like that doesn't shake you up, you can handle just about anything.

Another person on that flight was Ray Kroc, the man who made a fortune as CEO of McDonald's. When the plane landed, everybody was relieved to be alive. After that type of experience, you naturally bond with the people who went through it with you. Kroc, Irv, and I started talking, and Kroc was really impressed with Irv. Kroc spoke with Irv about the need to see more diversity ownership at his McDonald's restaurants. He basically told Irv that if he wanted a McDonald's franchise, it was as good as his, that he'd have one waiting.

That's the kind of impact Irv has on people. They gravitate to him. The best way to describe Irv is as a gem: a jewel of a guy. When you see him, you don't have to be extremely perceptive to know you're dealing with someone special.

The first time I met Irv was when he played at Northwestern. I was scouting for the Cowboys' first ever draft class of 1961. I talked to the coach at Northwestern, Ara Parseghian, and he spoke about Irv in glowing terms. After meeting Irv I was equally impressed. Parseghian was a no-nonsense coach who gave you the real deal with players. The way he talked about Irv, I knew he was a solid guy.

I had solid information on Irv before the 1961 draft, and we probably should have taken him. We didn't. That's something he hasn't let me forget. Our first draft pick ever was Bob Lilly, who turned out to be a Hall of Fame defensive tackle—at least I don't have to apologize to Irv for taking Bob!

Even so, Irv turned out to be a very good NFL player. Not a great player, but very good. I don't know if I would call him a shutdown corner by today's NFL standards, but he was one of the top cornerbacks in the league during his career. He was an all-around football player, just like he was an all-around person. He played special teams, he did everything, and he was tough.

When the Cowboys played the Eagles, we knew Irv was a guy you couldn't fool. He was too smart for that. The better I got to know Irv, the more I was impressed with him. The same was true of our coach, Tom Landry, and our general manager Tex Schramm.

We were so taken with Irv that after his NFL career ended, the Cowboys offered him a front office job. Not as general manager, but a front office job, with the anticipation that he would become a general manager one day.

There's no doubt in my mind Irv would have become the NFL's first black general manager if he had taken that job we offered him with the Cowboys in 1971. Our organization had stability. We had a track record of success. And Irv could have made a smooth transition from our front office to running the show with somebody else. Everyone he dealt with around the league would have been impressed with him. There's no doubt somebody would have tried to hire him away from us. He had everything—the NFL connections, the experience of being a player, scouting experience, a knack for finances, ability to handle the media, and knowledge of the game. It was easy for me to picture Irv running a draft, making a trade, or negotiating contracts. Tex felt the same way.

Unfortunately for us, Irv turned down our offer with the Cowboys and opted for a career with CBS. That turned out pretty good for him! When he landed on the *NFL Today* show with Brent Musberger and Phyllis George, I wasn't surprised. Irv is the kind of guy you want in the spotlight. He knew the game, and television had become a huge part of NFL business.

Irv had a great run on the *NFL Today* and he didn't have to worry about wins and losses! The guy is good at anything he does. He's going to do everything in a first class, professional way. When that show was on, it became habit-forming to watch. If you loved football and watched games on Sunday, it was the perfect way to start your day.

Much of Irv's life has been connected to the NFL, just like mine. I've met plenty of people during my six decades working in the NFL, and I still haven't met anyone nicer than Irv. More than that, he's a loyal friend. Whenever you see Irv, it's like running into your brother.

Irv never had anything handed to him. He earned it. I know some things about how he grew up. I know that he was one of fifteen children. I know his family wasn't exactly swimming in money.

Obviously I don't know everything about Irv, because we didn't grow up together and Irv rarely talks about things that aren't positive. But there's much more to Irv than that great smile of his. He cares about people and has empathy for them— probably because of how he grew up. Irv has been through obstacles, but considers himself fortunate, and he's one of those people who makes you feel good just being around him.

I've known Irv for almost sixty years, and he has always been a good person, one of my favorite people. Think about that. Ask anybody who knows Irv, and they'll tell you the same thing.

He's too modest to say the things I'm saying about him, but Irv has lived an extraordinary life. If he ever needed something, I'd do it for him, no questions asked. So when he asked me to write the foreword for this book, I couldn't say no.

We didn't draft Irv. I couldn't convince him to work for the Cowboys. But having Irv Cross as a friend is a blessing. This book is important to Irv, so I'm glad to help. Irv has lived an extraordinary life but, more importantly, he's an extraordinary person. I'm just glad he's my friend. In his life, and in his career, Irv Cross has done it the right way.

1

BEING LIKE JACKIE ROBINSON

HOW did it feel being the first African American full-time sports analyst on national television? It felt like everybody was watching.

The *NFL Today*, which launched in 1975, became the country's most popular pregame football show, and I was proud to be part of it. People on the West Coast woke up watching us. People on the East Coast rushed home from church to see us.

A lot of people were pulling for me when I got the *NFL Today* job. I also knew that some people were hoping I would stub my toe and wash out.

Either way, I didn't care. I was thrilled and I was ready. By the time I joined the groundbreaking *NFL Today* show in 1975, I had already been working at CBS for several years as an analyst and reporter. I knew that a national NFL pregame show would be a major step up in my career, but I was prepared. I was determined to make my parents proud, just like the great Jackie Robinson told me to do when I was a teenager.

I can't start this book without mentioning Robinson, one of my idols, whose life was a major inspiration to me. When Robinson broke the color barrier in major league baseball in 1947, I was just seven years old. I was too young to comprehend the significance of what Robinson was doing. That was long before I would even start to believe that I could play in the NFL one day.

However, Robinson's arrival into the major leagues was a game-changer that inspired a generation of black people. It certainly inspired my family. We used to crowd around the radio and listen to Dodgers games when Robinson played. Jackie was a hero, and of course I became a huge fan.

My participation in sports brought me face-to-face with Jackie Robinson years later, when I was still a teenager. I met Jackie at a baseball banquet when I was fifteen years old. By this time, playing in the NFL still seemed like a pipe dream, but I wanted to attend college. I was one of fifteen kids in my family, and nobody in my family had ever gone to college. I was a good student, and I was also gaining a reputation in Indiana as a pretty good athlete.

The banquet was in Chicago, which isn't too far from Hammond. I was one of the kids who had made the regional baseball All-Star team. So I caught a ride up to Chicago with a half-dozen other guys. I was sitting on the dais, and when I looked down to my right not too far away, there he was. Jackie Robinson in the flesh! As my future *NFL Today* colleague Brent Musberger might say, "I was looking live at Jackie Robinson!"

I was in seventh heaven; one of those moments when it felt like you were in a movie or dreaming. I remember like it was yesterday. Jackie had that white hair. He had that great smile. It was really him. And my heart was pounding!

I've come to realize how important it was for Jackie to do what he did that night—talking to young people, inspiring dreams. Jackie could have been doing something else that night. But in addition to being courageous, Jackie was generous. He gave of his time. He cared about others. Jackie wasn't just interested in accolades, in making things better for himself. He wanted to uplift those who hadn't come as far.

That's why Jackie Robinson remains a hero to me. I believe in the idea of giving back, of using your blessings to help others. That's what Jackie was about until the day he died.

"A life is not important except in the impact it has on other lives," is a Jackie Robinson quote.

It's one thing to be a great player. It's another to be a great person. Jackie was both.

Jackie knew all the kids he spoke to that night in Chicago were not destined to play major league baseball. In fact, it was more likely that none of us would become professional ballplayers. But he was willing to talk with us, a group of young, energetic, and impressionable kids who were thrilled to be in the same room with him. He was the most famous person I had ever met up to that point. Heck, he was the only famous person I had ever met. I didn't have a crystal ball to see my future, when I would be interviewing athletes in their living rooms, covering Super Bowls, or playing in NFL games myself on Sunday afternoons. Who would have imagined all that back then? Certainly not me.

Jackie gave a pretty good speech, at least I remember it that way. He had probably done hundreds of them just like it. But what he said after his speech ended really moved me. He came over and shook hands with all the kids that were there. When he shook hands with me, he looked at me and said, "Son, whatever you do in life, make your parents proud."

I never forgot what a deep impression Jackie Robinson's words had on me. Maybe it's because the great Jackie Robinson was saying it. Maybe it was because my mother died when I was ten years old, and I had missed her ever since. Either way, it definitely stuck with me.

But the idea of making my parents proud resonated with me. I knew my family wasn't the same as many families. I had friends who had both parents living at home. My mom had died. Most of my friends didn't have fourteen brothers and sisters. I did. As I got older, taking care of my younger brothers and sisters became part of my routine, just like my older brothers and sisters had done for me.

It was already clear to me early on that I needed a plan for what I wanted to do in life. That didn't frighten me or intimidate me. In fact, I already had a plan. I was going to be the first person from my family to go to college, and to graduate. Maybe I would be a coach, or a teacher, but I was going to make something of myself, and do it the honest way.

That meant I had to be disciplined. That meant I couldn't give up when the odds were stacked against me. That meant I couldn't let my goals be defined by stereotypes that others may have believed.

You know the old saying among many black people. You had to be better and hungrier to get what came easier for someone else. I believed that. Coming from where I came from, I lived that every day.

When I was doing the *NFL Today*, the spirit of Jackie Robinson was always with me. I was going to work harder than anybody else. I was going to know more about pro football than anybody. If things didn't work out, it wouldn't be because I wasn't prepared.

As it turned out, things worked out pretty well for me. In my opinion, the *NFL Today* is still the standard by which NFL pregame shows are measured. On the air, we had a chemistry that just clicked. We were all so different, yet it worked. We had Brent Musburger, the smooth, polished television guy who could set everyone up. We had Phyllis George, a former Miss America, beautiful and smart, who attracted an entirely different audience, including women. We had Jimmy "The Greek" Snyder, a character, a gambler, who made us even more edgy. For two years while Phyllis was gone we had Jayne Kennedy, a pioneer in her own right, a wonderful person and a beautiful black woman who, in my opinion, should have been treated better than she was.

And then we had me, a former NFL player who knew the game inside out, and who had TV experience, and who was determined not to fail. As an African American, I was getting an opportunity that was unique for that time, and my presence helped bring a more diverse audience.

As you know, things on The *NFL Today* weren't always perfect. There were battles between Jimmy and Brent. There was tension between Phyllis and Jimmy. And of course, there was the famous meltdown by The Greek, when he rambled offensively about black athletes while he was being interviewed at a restaurant. That mistake cost Jimmy everything—his job, his reputation, his life.

Decades later, I can look back at the good times and bad times in my life with few regrets. On camera, I always gave it my best effort, just like when I played in the NFL. I can watch tapes of those shows and still be proud. I wasn't a showman or a clown. I did my job. I was me. I bore the cross.

I don't refer to myself as a pioneer in television, but others have. A ton of ex-athletes, black athletes, are working for networks these days. But in 1975, when the *NFL Today* was launched, the sports TV landscape looked much different, much whiter. I never focused on that, but I was keenly aware that if I failed, it might be a long time before another black person got a similar opportunity.

Every time I see James Brown or Greg Gumbel or Tom Jackson on national television, I take pride, knowing that in some way, large or small, I helped create an avenue for them. Many people helped me. God was always with me. For that, I am forever grateful.

Since I left television, I've spent many Sundays at church, so I'm hardly an expert on all the current network pregame shows. I'm at a different stage in my life. I'm writing this memoir at seventy-seven years old, and I know my time on this earth is growing short. I have great memories. I've had a great life. But I've also lost many great friends, and I realize that nothing lasts forever, including this body of mine that feels the pain of playing nine years in the NFL.

That's part of the reason I decided to do this book. I thought about it for years, but always had something taking up my time. I was never one to sit still and reflect on the ups and downs in my life. I also have never craved attention, nor did I enjoy talking about myself.

For me, the quiet moments in my life are often an opportunity for prayer. I want to get closer to God, to find my purpose, to figure out how he wants me to use the rest of my life. Somehow, when I thought about those things, the idea of telling my story and sharing it with others wouldn't go away. Maybe some good would come of it. Maybe I was wasting an opportunity by keeping my story to myself.

Finally, I realized I shouldn't wait any longer if I was going to do a book. I've run into former NFL players who are my age, or younger, who were world beaters when they played. Now they're in wheelchairs, their bodies broken. Or their minds are broken, unable to remember precise moments, or even to recognize their loved ones.

I believe God has a purpose and plan for all of us. I think often about my purpose, and what God wants me to do. What can I do to live the life God has placed me on this earth to live? All my life, I've wanted to be of service, to make a difference. It comes from my Christian faith.

Maybe this book is part of that purpose. Maybe it will inspire some people to find their purpose. Jackie Robinson inspired me by sharing a message with me that I never forgot.

When people recognize me today, they often say, "Hey Irv, where have you been?"

Now I can simply respond, "Read my book."

Here it is. I hope you enjoy it. And if it brings you closer to finding God's plan for you, well, that's even better.

2

MOM, DAD, AND
DOMESTIC VIOLENCE

MY father used to beat my mother.

Obviously, that's a part of my childhood I don't discuss openly with people when I meet them, or even after I've known them for many years. The pain of that is still there, more than sixty years after it occurred. It was violent and it was scary.

I was brought to tears when I tapped into those memories for this book. I loved my mother. I loved my father. I love my entire family, all of my brothers and sisters.

That only makes the memories I have of my mom's suffering harder to take. And obviously, I wish she had lived much longer than she did.

Before I speak about the abuse, let me talk more about how I grew up.

We had plenty of love and caring in our household, despite my dad's issues with alcohol. As I mentioned, there were fifteen kids in my family. That's a lot of mouths to feed and we were poor. I'm the middle kid, No. 8. There were seven kids above me and seven kids younger than me—eight boys and seven girls.

It's fascinating how we all had different personalities. I was probably most similar to my younger brother Ray. He'll tell you he's a better athlete than me, and he's right. That love for sports was a constant bond between us.

Meanwhile my older brother Jimmy and I were almost opposites. I wouldn't call Jimmy a hell-raiser, but if there was some action going on somewhere, he was close to the scene. He started smoking at a very early age. If Jimmy saw a cigarette butt in an ashtray, he'd take it out and smoke it.

Jimmy started doing this when he was like ten years old. He died of a lung condition several years ago, and before he passed, he had to wear an oxygen mask.

Jimmy had a little bit of my father in him. He would get drunk on weekends, raise a little hell.

He'd get in a barfight or two. If you had a difference of opinion with Jimmy, he'd stand in front of you until he proved he was right. Saying he was wrong wasn't one of Jimmy's strengths. If you disagreed with Jimmy, you might get punched in the nose. But he served in the military as well, and made a life for himself.

I was really the first one in my family to participate in sports because of my friend Herbie Ruffin, whose father loved Jackie Robinson. With that many people in the house, responsibilities had to be delegated among all of us, particularly the older children. My older brothers and sisters didn't have hours of free time to play outside, to enjoy their childhood the way kids from smaller families could.

Mom and Dad just couldn't do it all by themselves, especially since Mom was often pregnant with the next child. So the older brothers and sisters helped take care of the younger brothers and sisters.

The girls slept in the front bedroom upstairs, and the boys slept in the middle room downstairs. There were usually five of us to a bed, as we only had a couple. Three of us slept at the top of the bed, two of us slept at the bottom.

I think I had a brand new pair of shoes once in my childhood. Everything else was a hand-me-down from older brothers and sisters. We had chores as soon as you were old enough to handle some.

I had to get up early in the morning to take care of the coal stove. I usually got up at five o'clock. I had to start the fire and have the house warm before everybody woke up. We had coal delivered to the house, dropped on the sidewalk, and I took it to the basement. Years later when I was grown, I went back to visit the house I grew up in. The house seemed so much smaller than it did when I was a kid. It has since been torn down, and the last time I was there it was nothing but an open lot.

I honestly don't have many vivid memories of being hungry. Somehow, my Dad and the older siblings were resourceful enough to get us all enough to eat. Usually we had plenty of food. My father walked back and forth to work. He'd pass a chicken house and a butcher shop along the way. The butcher was owned by this Polish guy, and my father would sometimes come home with fresh cuts of meats that he purchased from the butcher.

We'd usually have Cream of Wheat or oatmeal or cereal for breakfast. I never felt like I missed a lot of meals. I do remember some days at school, when we had milk and cookies during a break, that I'd be real happy. I guess those must have been days when I felt like I really didn't get enough to eat.

My dad was a hunter and he also liked to fish. To him, this was more than just recreation.

Those skills helped provide for us. All of my older brothers hunted and fished with my father. I was the oddball. I didn't go, because I didn't believe in killing anything. I felt that way as a child and it still hasn't changed. I've never gone hunting and I've only been fishing a couple of times. The only part I regret is that by not going hunting or fishing, I missed out on spending more time with my father.

After one of father's successful hunting excursions, a wide variety of cuisine would make its way to the Cross dinner table. You can imagine that wasting food wasn't an option at the Cross household. You ate everything on your plate, and you were grateful you had a plate. Because we couldn't be picky about what we ate, we'd eat odd things, at least odd to me, like squirrel, rabbit, racoon. I didn't especially like racoon, but I ate it because I had to. My mom would fix it up and she was a good cook, but I just never took a liking to some of those exotic dishes. If I didn't like something, I'd put a small portion on my plate. We had two tables where we ate. The older kids sat at one table, and the younger kids ate at a table in the kitchen. My father sat with the older kids, and one of my older sisters would sit with the young kids, making sure they ate and behaved. My father was a terrific guitar player—learned by ear. I remember sitting around with my family, my father playing guitar, and a couple of my sisters had great singing voices.

The concept of sharing was instilled in me early. There was no such thing as my room, my food, my toy. Everything was "ours."

There's no way I could ever eat something, or have something, without thinking about my brothers and sisters, and what they might need.

If I had two pieces of anything to eat, one piece went to a brother or sister. If I had a Twinkie, I would bring it home and share it. Our clothes were handed down. We supported one another.

I've never understood people who obviously had more than they needed, but weren't willing to give. I've always thought giving should be part of a person's makeup, the ability to share willingly with others.

One of my first jobs was setting pins at a bowling alley a couple of nights a week. I made $5.75 for the week I think. There was a White Castle restaurant right across the street from the bowling alley. For 75 cents, you'd get maybe a dozen White Castle hamburgers.

I'd come home from work after payday, put $5 on the table for my father, and I'd take a sack of hamburgers up with me and give them to my brothers and sisters. That's what life was like for us, and it has carried over into adulthood for me. I've never been driven by material things, I guess because I did without them growing up. Having six or seven overcoats never made sense to me. When I have extra things, I know it's time to start giving stuff away.

Now for the difficult part—talking about the domestic violence. While we were all taking care of each other, my father spent many long hours at work. He usually got up around 5:30 and walked to work. Rain, snow, it didn't matter. He just went. There was work all over the place in Hammond, Indiana, and that's how my father, and my family, ended up there. There were a million jobs in Hammond, East Chicago, Gary, and Chicago. Steel mills and oil refineries were close by. If you were a carpenter or electrician, if you had that kind of skill set and worked there all your life, you could end up with a decent income and a nice pension plan, and at the very least you could raise your family. At that time, you were looking at steady work for forty or fifty years. My father worked in a scrap iron company where he would burn parts. It was a tough job. You worked outside, even if it was 25 degrees below zero.

Most of the black people in Hammond lived on our side of town, but our immediate neighborhood was integrated. My next-door neighbor was Polish and his father owned a bakery. A lot of people in my neighborhood were from Eastern Europe. Everybody in Hammond knew my father. Our family was one of the first African American families in town.

My father never had any trouble with the law, except when he drank. Dad did a good job providing for his family, but he had this drinking problem. In the bar he used to go to, there was this poolroom. The guys would shoot pool, and they would gamble. Then he'd come home and that's when the trouble would start.

I hated what happened on Fridays. That's when my father got paid. That's when my father drank. Old Grandad whiskey, that was his drink. It was like clockwork. He'd cash his paycheck, give my mother most of the money, but he'd take a few bucks, then head to the tavern and get drunk. He'd come back and beat Mom up. You knew every Friday night that something was going to happen—something bad.

This was where my dislike for alcohol started. I saw how drinking changed my father's personality into something ugly. I saw how he couldn't control his actions when under the influence of alcohol. I saw things I never wanted to see, things no child should have to see.

My father certainly wasn't alone in his behavior. Alcohol has taken the same stranglehold over millions of people. It has shattered families and ruined lives. At some point during my adolescence I decided I would never be a drinker, and I have kept that vow throughout my life.

As a hunter, my father had a shotgun, and sometimes he'd fill that thing up with bullets, go out on the back porch, and fire that shotgun. I was afraid he was going to shoot somebody by accident—drunk, stumbling, and shooting a gun. The police came by a few times and made him stop. Once, they even took him to jail, let him dry out, and brought him back home.

My father's behavior when drunk was such an odd thing, because with the kids, he was never abusive. He treated my mother so badly but he was good with all the kids. However, my father had an old school mentality about life. The father was supposed to set the law. When he said "No," that was it. He felt the father was the head of the family, and his word was the last word. You don't challenge him. When we talked to him, we addressed him as "Yes sir, no sir."

Maybe my mother challenged him sometimes, I don't know. But I still remember those nights when he hit my mother with horror. I wasn't even ten years old, and I felt helpless. There was a big easy chair in the living room. When my father would beat her, I would hide behind that chair and sulk when she was beaten. A couple of times, some of my brothers tried to jump on my father's back in an attempt to intervene. But he was much stronger than us.

When I was ten years old, my mother died during childbirth.

I didn't know what was going on at first. I came out of our bedroom the next morning and went downstairs, and my mother wasn't in my parents' room. But the baby was there.

I said, "Where's Little Ma?" That's what we called my mother. My grandmother was "Big Ma."

My mother was gone, having passed away during the night. I've always thought that the way my father beat my mother may have had something to do with her death. She had varicose veins and problems with that, but I think the physical abuse that she took accelerated her health problems. She had a baby every year, and maybe with the beatings and the babies, it was simply too much for her to take.

Whatever the case, she was gone. Losing her like that left a mark that still hurts to this day.

However, something else happened the day my mother died. That same day, my father stopped drinking—cold turkey, and forever.

My father didn't take a drop of liquor the rest of his life. He lived to be eighty-six years old, and for about the last forty-five years, he was completely sober. I never asked him why he stopped drinking, and he never told me why. Was it guilt? Was it grief? Was it fear that if he didn't stop drinking, he would lose his family after already losing his wife? I'll never know, but after my mother died, my father and alcohol parted ways.

Meanwhile we were all left with the pain of my mother's death. Losing your mother at any age can be traumatic, but especially when you are a young child. I'm sure it has affected me, with the way I've dealt with certain things in my life. Fortunately, I studied some psychology when I got to Northwestern, and I've learned about human nature and how we respond to certain things.

I really missed my mother, but I wasn't close to her the way some kids are close to their mother. I was close from the standpoint that she fed me, took care of me, and loved me. But in my family, before you knew it, another kid was coming along. That cuddling, that one-on-one warmth you have with a mother, where you can feel her heartbeat, her caress? I didn't have a lot of that. She couldn't hold me for that long, because there would be another child to take care of. You wind up not being handled that much. In some ways, you're on your own.

I've always been a bit of a loner, and I think that's one reason why. I often felt alone growing up, even in a house with that many people. When I was young, I wasn't an easy person to get to know. I'd go hours without speaking. There were so many people in my house, I was shy, and I'd end up just listening, not saying a word. In a crowded room, I was never the center of attention. It's kind of ironic that someone who doesn't like attention ended up being on national television, being a broadcaster for a living.

In my television career, it helped that I was a good listener. It made people feel comfortable that I let them talk, and during interviews it helped them to open up more than they ordinarily would have.

One of my most memorable *NFL Today* interviews was one I did with Dexter Manley, the former Redskins defensive end who reached the NFL without being able to read. For years, Dexter fooled people, bringing the newspaper into the locker room when he couldn't even tell you what it said. Even his wife didn't know he couldn't read.

At first Dexter didn't want me to interview him about his inability to read. He was embarrassed and didn't want to relive some of the pain. Dexter had a learning disability and kids made fun of him throughout his childhood, called him dumb and demeaned him in various ways because he didn't do well in school. But as Dexter and I got to know each other we developed a relationship. He finally opened up and talked about it. After the interview, I received letters from viewers, saying how much they were moved by his experience. Meanwhile, Dexter took classes that improved his reading ability from the second grade level to the tenth grade. For the first time in his life he could actually understand what was in the newspaper that he once used as a prop to hide his secret.

Revealing a secret helped Dexter, so in this chapter, I have opened up to you about my childhood, and about what I saw my mother go through. When I joined the *NFL Today*, and remained on the show for over a decade, millions of people were watching. I just wish my Mom could have been one of them.

If there's anyone out there who's in a similar situation, dealing with domestic violence, seek help. Unlike my mom's situation, maybe your situation can change before it's too late.

3

DAD SAVES THE FAMILY

I'LL never forget the day child services came to our house. Their intention was to break up my family.

It was shortly after my mother died. Apparently, there was some question about how my father, now a widower, would be able to take care of so many kids by himself.

The people from child services had all of my brothers and sisters lined up against the wall, oldest to youngest. This lady was going to assign my brothers and sisters to different houses with different families. All these official-looking cars were lined up outside. They weren't police cars, but to me, they looked like police cars. They were intimidating, ominous.

Apparently some other families had already agreed to take us. I'm not sure if it was going to be a part-time arrangement or full-time.

At some point, thank God, my father came home from work while they were still at the house. I'm sure they had spoken to him about this before, but maybe he thought it was over. Maybe he thought he had reassured these people that he was capable of handling things.

My father was family-oriented, and so was my grandfather. They believed you took care of your kids, somehow, someway. I know that's what he was thinking—"I'm not giving up any of my kids. I brought them in here. I'm going to take care of them."

He saw himself as being responsible for his kids. They must have tried to talk my father into thinking differently. You know, saying stuff like, "We have these agencies that can come in. They can provide a better life for your kids."

I'm sure my father was still grieving over his wife's death. It was a shock to us all. I can't imagine some of the things that were going through his mind. When you're under that kind of stress, and you've had to deal with a tragedy, you can be vulnerable. Maybe somewhere in the back of his mind, he wondered if we would be better off in another situation. I never talked to him about it, so I'm not sure exactly what transpired before those people showed up at our door.

With so many kids, there's no way they planned to send all my brothers and sisters to one family. They were going to split us up, spread us all over town, or maybe even further away. There was a family right across the street that had some foster care kids. Maybe a few of us would've gone over there.

I was scared. As a matter of fact, I was crying. I didn't understand everything that was going on. But I knew they were talking about splitting us up, that all of us weren't going to end up in the same place. I had already lost my mother. I didn't want to lose more of my family.

Whatever the case, when my father came home, he wasn't having this. He was furious.

I remember him yelling at this woman, standing in our house.

"Nobody's going to break up this family," he said. There was some more conversation between my father and the child services people, but father was adamant. Nobody was taking his kids. The woman and those people left. All my brothers and sisters stayed.

That was a close call, but it never happened again. That's when my older brothers and sisters started rotating, staying home from school to take care of the youngest kids in the family. When I got older, it became my turn to stay home from school, once a week, to care for my siblings. Those days when I stayed home from school went fast, I guess because I was so busy. I had to make sure my younger brothers and sisters were fed. I wasn't much of a cook, but my sisters usually had something fixed in the refrigerator that I could give to the kids.

The toughest job was settling whatever sibling disputes came up before my father came home. You know how brothers and sisters are. I didn't spank them, but I had to discipline them. Diapers had to be changed. I also had to make sure that my younger siblings who had chores actually did them.

We also had friends who looked out for us. One of the church ladies used to come over and fix meals for us. I don't know if my father had any sort of special relationship with her or not. But she was there a lot for dinner, too.

With no mother and so many siblings, I knew how important it was to have a job, and to earn money, especially being a man. All my older brothers worked, and frankly, there was pressure on the older boys to get out of the house as soon as they finished high school. Whether you got a job or went into the military, you were expected to get out on your own right away and to provide for yourself. My three oldest brothers all went to the military right out of high school.

My oldest brother was a Navy man and served in World War II. I had an older sister who became a nurse. Some of my other older brother and sisters were already out of the house when I got to be a teenager, so I assumed their responsibilities of working when I could, and doing what I could for the family.

I had so many jobs growing up, I've probably forgotten a few. I remember doing cleanup work at a doctor's office in town. Actually, that was my mother's job, but I came with her. She got the idea I might grow up to be a doctor one day. "Dr. Cross," she'd say smiling. That's a nice memory.

I did it all, shoveling snow, running errands for people, whatever I could to bring in money. And the money I brought home, I gave to my father.

"When Irv worked at night, he'd buy doughnuts at this bakery across the street and bring them home to us," my younger brother Ray has said. "We slept in the attic upstairs. He'd come home and shake me out of my sleep. He'd put his hand up to his mouth and say, 'Shuh. Don't tell anybody.' We'd have doughnuts and ice cream before we went back to sleep. We were a poor family but we were a happy family.

"I remember this night when it was so cold in the attic, you could blow your breath and see smoke. Irv came home tired from work and got on the bed. But the bed broke in about three places and hit the floor. I heard Irv say, 'Aw shoot.' I was laughing. That's one of the few times I remember him getting mad about something. I knew he had to be tired, and he just wanted to go to sleep. Irv just grabbed the covers off the bed, rolled onto the floor, and slept there all night. We did what we had to do."

I never got in trouble for missing school on days when I had to stay home to take care of my brothers and sisters. The school knew why I wasn't there, and nobody at the school ever talked to me about it.

There was a lot of love and sacrifice in our household and we made it work. So many kids today are products of broken homes, which can make finding your direction in life that much tougher.

I was particularly close to Ray, who was actually a better athlete than I was. Ray was on the Hammond High team that won the Indiana state championship in 1960, and he also played running back and defensive back, and ran track. Ray earned a scholarship to Western New Mexico St., and he was captain of both the football and track teams.

The Atlanta Falcons signed Ray as a free agent, but he tore up his knee shortly after that and could never get over that injury. But Ray didn't let that stop his life from being a success. He returned to Hammond and became a successful teacher and coach. In 2001, Ray was inducted into the Hammond Sports Hall of Fame. I was inducted into that same Hall of Fame in 1987, and I think it's pretty neat that Ray and I will be together there forever.

It seems like everybody in Hammond loves and respects Ray as much as I do. They should. He's a great man. I'd like to think some of the things I passed along to Ray helped him in life. He may not have needed it, as strong as he was. But I'm glad I was there to provide him with somebody to look at who loved him, and who was trying to give him a role model to follow. It's great to have role models outside your home, but I wanted to give Ray a role model that he could see every day.

"I don't go around announcing to people that Irv is my brother," Ray said. "I'm just not built that way. I've always stood on my own two feet, and I've wanted people to accept me for who I am. So when people find out, they always say, 'Why didn't you tell me you were Irv's brother?'

"That's funny, but you better believe I'm proud of him. The first black sports analyst on national TV. The first black analyst to get the Pete Rozelle Award from the Hall of Fame. Irv did it with pride. No bling, no glitter, all substance. He showed the way for everyone who came after him.

"Irv hasn't forgotten where he came from. I've been teaching school for years in Hammond now, so I tell him what's going on back here, and he has helped his family and other people.

"The only advice I have for Irv is that he needs to get rid of that part in his hair. He's almost eighty years old, now. C'mon man. But my father was the same way. He had that part, too."

I'm so glad my family stayed together after my mother died. When you have seven younger siblings like I do, it's natural to have a sense of nurturing and protecting. I think that has made me a more caring person. When I see kids coming from difficult situations, I see my family. When I see kids in programs like Big Brothers and Big Sisters, I see my family.

If we had been split up, so many things would have been different. The memories we have. The relationships we have. Our closeness to each other. And who knows what it would have done to my father?

My father lived to be eighty-six years old, long enough to watch me on the *NFL Today*. He could walk around town with his chest poked out. My entire family could.

I'm the oldest boy who's still alive, and I'm grateful our family had the strength to overcome the challenges that faced us—together. It's part of what makes me who I am.

4

MY FIRST MENTOR, MISS EWING

MY career in television would have never happened without Ruth Ewing, my fifth-grade teacher at Maywood Elementary School in Hammond, Indiana.

After my mother passed away, I'm sure there were people worried about my family. What would happen to us with all of those children? Would we be properly cared for? Could my father handle doing it by himself as a single parent?

Miss Ewing was among those who worried about me. But she never expressed her concern with pity. She did what she did best. She taught me, not only with academic lessons, but life lessons.

Originally from South Dakota, where she grew up as a next-door neighbor to former vice president Hubert Humphrey, she moved to Hammond after college and became a favorite teacher for generations of students, teaching at Maywood for over thirty years, from 1937 to 1968.

That's an incredible run in the same town, doing the same thing, and Hammond was blessed to have her. She had a genuine concern for kids. According to an article written about her in the

Times of Northwest Indiana, Miss Ewing never had a day when she didn't love work. I believe her. That's how it seemed when you were one of her students. If there was something going on with you, if you weren't responding in class the way she wanted, she'd find out why. She had a heart of gold, and really cared about all of her students.

Another segment of the newspaper article described Miss Ewing's personality perfectly:

"It was not unusual for her to start a school day with, 'I smell Juicy Fruit Gum! Anyone chewing gum can deposit it in the waste basket now!' When winter colds were prevalent, she might begin the class with, 'I think we might need to do a little postural drainage exercise. Put your head on your desk face down for a few minutes and clear your nose.'"

Miss Ewing was strict, no doubt about it. But she also had a wonderful demeanor—pleasant face, glasses, with a great smile. She was a person who could show compassion with strength and guidance. Later in life I had a coach like that in college at Northwestern, Ara Parseghian. Coach Parseghian wasn't about nonsense, but he taught you something every day if you paid attention. The same was true with Miss Ewing.

She didn't want to be your friend, not when you were a child, and she was the teacher. She was a mentor in the greatest sense. She wanted to help mold kids into better students, and better people.

Thinking back to those days, it's kind of incredible I ended up speaking on national television for a living. Coming from a big family like mine, there would be times when I'd sit in a crowded room all day and never say a word. You wouldn't even know I was there. My parents would talk freely, as would my siblings, especially the older ones. But not me. I was always the quiet one.

Part of that silence was due to the things that transpired between my mother and father on those awful Friday nights. I had internalized a lot of that. I didn't know how to express myself or handle those feelings, so I was introverted.

The period following my mother's death was critical for me, although I was too young to realize it. There was a strong possibility that I could have become even more withdrawn and slipped further into isolation. My confidence and self-esteem were in a fragile place.

Miss Ewing's kindness and interest in me kept me grounded and helped me blossom. It was obvious that I was more depressed than normal, but even though she was aware my mother had died, she never spoke directly to me about that. Instead, she focused on bringing out my best qualities, things I didn't even realize were deep within me.

She came over to my seat one day, and every time I tell this story, I can see it like it happened yesterday. She put her arm around me and said, "You're the kind of young man who can go to college."

I was thinking, *College?* Nobody in my family had ever gone to college. Graduating from high school was the ultimate educational goal. You'd go from there to the steel mill, or maybe into the service. But going to college? That wasn't how we thought.

Miss Ewing changed that for me. She kept telling me I could do it. It didn't happen instantly, but over weeks and months, Miss Ewing's vision of me going to college became my vision as well. That was a key turning point in my life, because I knew if I could get to college, it would open doors for me that reached far beyond Hammond—doors that would be closed without education.

As part of her class, we had a pretend radio station with the call letters "WGCR." The "GCR" stood for Good Citizens Room. Miss Ewing made me the managing editor of the station, which was really a mop bucket and broomstick, with a piece of cardboard atop the broomstick serving as the microphone. That was a long way from CBS studios in New York!

Every Friday morning, you had to give your report on the station in front of the class. Miss Ewing was really teaching us public speaking and writing, as you had to write your report out and it had to be organized. I found myself really looking forward to those Friday mornings. As managing editor I was introducing people, and I was giving my own reports, too.

The fact that Miss Ewing selected me as managing editor made me feel special. Getting praise for the job I was doing gave me confidence, especially when the praise came from Miss Ewing.

My improved self-esteem started to carry over into outside the classroom. Now when people approached me, I was feeling more self-assured. I was talking more. I used to look down at the floor when I spoke to people, especially grownups. All they would see was the top of my head. Now I was making eye contact and talking to people without that knot in my stomach. It felt great.

Miss Ewing also changed my study habits. She said, "Irv, always make sure you do your homework." Coming to Miss Ewing's class without my homework done was an unfathomable thought. So my routine was to leave school, and go straight to the library to do my homework, before I even came home. I was fortunate the library was close to my home, and there was a field between the back of my house and the library that you could use for a shortcut. Our house was a rough place to study, plenty of distractions. The library became my sanctuary.

Because I was doing my homework, I was getting good grades. And that reinforced my confidence even more. Miss Ewing kept feeding into that, raising the bar for me, setting new goals and exposing me to different things.

I still remember Miss Ewing entering me in the city spelling bee. I wanted to win it so badly, but I finished second. The word that knocked me out was "receive." I spelled it "r-e-c-i-e-v-e." The second after I said it, I knew it was wrong. Of course, the next person spelled it correctly right away. I was disappointed. But the bigger victory was that I was so self-assured during that competition, in front of everybody. It was another example that huge victories can be learned in defeat. I wanted to win the spelling bee, but the victory was that I had come out of my shell.

Without Miss Ewing, I truly believe I would have never found the confidence to express myself publicly. When her class ended, she gave me a summer reading list. I spent most of that summer in the library, reading one book and then another. My horizons were expanding outside of Hammond. That's one of the many beauties of reading. It takes your mind to another place. Have you ever become so immersed in a book that you forget where you are, that you become oblivious to everything else around you? I was experiencing that feeling for the first time, and I was fascinated.

Hours upon hours passed that summer, as I traveled to different places through those library books. While other kids were outside playing, I was learning about the library catalogue system and how to find books myself. When one book was finished, it was on to the next adventure.

"Irv was reserved," Ray Cross said. "If you didn't know he was in the room, you might overlook him. He was constantly reading. When I was out playing basketball, or chasing girls, Irv was educating himself. Many times when I'd come in from playing outside, I'd see Irv standing in front of a mirror, looking into it and talking to himself. The first time I saw that, I said, 'Daddy, what's wrong with Irv? He's talking to himself in the mirror?' My Daddy said, 'Leave him alone, leave him alone.'

"But you know I didn't. So I asked Irv, 'What are you doing man?' He called me 'Duff.'

"He said, 'Duff, there's no telling what I might be doing one day. I might be a radio announcer or something.'

You're talking about a black kid maybe fifteen years old, standing in front of a mirror in Hammond, Indiana. He had his notes, he was working on his speech. That's foresight. I was thinking about today, or tomorrow. He was thinking ten, twenty years ahead."

Spending all that time in the library helped me years later when I was a student at Northwestern. Something about the library just made me feel comfortable. At Northwestern, a lot of people never saw me other than at classes and at football practice. I found this place down in the bowels of the library where I could study. It was an enclosed area with no windows. But that was my special spot. There were some grad students down in that area, and they were all business. They had their routine and I had mine. I'd get in my little hole in the library and be down there all day.

I'm happy to say that Miss Ewing lived into her nineties. In fact, when that *Times of Northwest Indiana* article was written about Miss Ewing, she was about to turn ninety-three years old. She mentioned me in the article as one of her students that she was most proud of. When I read that, I felt like I was back in her fifth grade class again, so happy to earn her approval.

With Miss Ewing's direction, I became a serious student before I became a serious athlete. Even after I became a serious athlete, I remained a serious student. I can't thank her enough for that. I've seen so many athletes waste the opportunity of having a free ride to college. It was never going to be that way for me. I was a student first, an athlete second. Even when my athletic achievements began to create opportunities, I had no interest in attending a university that wasn't going to benefit me academically. Obviously, I grew up in a different era when being a Pro Bowl player didn't bring you a multi-million dollar contract. But in any era, education had value. It still does. Higher education was something I wanted to experience.

For me, Miss Ewing planted the seed for that way of thinking. Instead of choosing to work in one of the mills around Hammond, I decided I wanted a different path. I still wasn't exactly sure how I was going to accomplish that, but Miss Ewing spotted potential in me early, and I was not going to let my family tragedy defeat me. Miss Ewing was everything a teacher is supposed to be, and I've talked to other former students of Miss Ewing who were also enriched for life by her class.

Years after I had left Hammond, when I was doing the *NFL Today* show, I got a chance to talk to Miss Ewing again. She called one of my sisters who put her in touch with me. Miss Ewing had always been a huge sports fan, and she was particularly passionate about following the Chicago White Sox. You'd see her at basketball games at Hammond High, cheering us on.

When I picked up the phone I still recognized her voice. She was living in a nursing home in Indiana. She told me that she watched me on TV, which was flattering to me, but did not surprise me. I'm thankful she didn't point out some mistakes I had made on the air recently, and I was thrilled to hear from her.

I told her, "Miss Ewing, I can't tell you how much you mean to me. None of this would have happened without you."

It was great to hear her voice. I wish I had called Miss Ewing more often through the years.

She has since passed away, but at least I got the chance to thank Miss Ewing for everything she had done, and for teaching me so well. She had confidence in me before I did, even telling me that I'd be going to college when the thought wasn't even in my mind. I owe it all to her.

5

MY FAITH

WHEN people ask me why I always seem calm, why I always stay positive in my thinking, I answer with two words— my faith.

Almost every morning, I start my day with Bible study. On days when I don't do that, like when I'm rushing to catch a plane or I'm late for an appointment, I don't feel right. Throughout the entire day, something seems a little bit off.

My faith keeps me grounded. Prayer keeps me close to God.

Here is my faith statement that I wrote in 2011. It serves as my words to live by:

My Faith Statement

I believe that Jesus Christ is the unique Son of God. He came to earth as a man to complete God's plan for the salvation of mankind. I know that he suffered excruciating pain and humiliation, took on the sins of the entire world, died on the cross, was resurrected, and ascended into heaven so that all who believe in Him and accept Him as their Lord and Savior will have eternal life.

I know God loves me unconditionally and has a wonderful plan for my life. I know man is sinful and separated from God because of sin. I know Jesus Christ is God's only provision for man's sin, and through Him I know and experience God's mercy and love. I have received Jesus Christ as my Lord and Savior and I know that, with the help of the Holy Spirit living in me, I can do God's will and accomplish great things for His kingdom.

I study the Bible daily and regularly attend Bible study classes, church, and Sunday school. My life is driven by Christ's command to love God with all my heart, soul, and mind and to love others as myself.

It is my faith that drives me to serve others as I follow the path God has placed before me. My goal is to love God with my whole heart and grow closer to Him every day, to recognize and follow His will for my life, confess my sins and repent, to have a heart like His, and to give Him praise and bring Him glory every day of my life.

God put me on this earth to serve my fellowman. I give God the glory for every single life he allows me to touch.

Irv Cross

5/31/11

I try to live in a way that God would want me to. My attitude is formed by the serenity prayer, written by Reinhold Niebuhr:

God, give us grace to accept with serenity
the things that cannot be changed,

Courage to change the things
which should be changed,
and the wisdom to distinguish
the one from the other.

Living one day at a time,
Enjoying one moment at a time,
Accepting hardship as a pathway to peace,
Taking, as Jesus did,
This sinful world as it is,
Not as I would have it,
Trusting that You will make all things right,
If I surrender to Your will,
So that I may be reasonably happy in this life,
And supremely happy with You forever in the next.
Amen.

From the first time I heard it, I wanted to know more about this prayer. There's such wisdom in it. Reading Niebuhr's prayer keeps me connected to what's going on in my life each day.

It didn't surprise me when I learned that Dr. Martin Luther King was also a big fan of Niebuhr's. Dr. King invited Niebuhr to the Selma-to-Montgomery protest march in 1965, but Niebuhr could not attend due to failing health.

"Only a severe stroke prevents me from accepting," Niebuhr wrote to Dr. King in a telegram. "I hope there will be a massive demonstration of all the citizens with conscious in favor of the elemental human rights of voting and freedom of assembly."

I would have loved to meet Niebuhr, and I have tried to adopt the serenity that his prayer describes.

Life isn't always easy, but my faith and belief in God never waver. My introduction to religion began when I was very young. Growing up in Hammond, I went to church all day on Sunday.

My grandmother actually wanted me to become a Methodist minister. Maybe she saw that side of me early. Maybe it was because I stayed out of trouble. I broke a window once growing up, and that's the only thing I remember getting in trouble for. We were playing baseball in the backyard, and I threw a pitch that got away! We stopped playing baseball in the backyard after that!

I enjoyed going to church. My father was Baptist. Both my grandmother and mother were Methodist. I had an uncle who was a pastor at what I called a "sanctified" church.

The service at the Methodist church started earlier than the Baptist church. I'd go to the Methodist church for Sunday school at nine o'clock followed by the eleven o'clock morning service. Then I'd run about eight blocks in my Sunday best to the Baptist church for the one o'clock afternoon service. Then in the evening I'd go to the sanctified church with my uncle at around four or five in the afternoon. There was lots of energy in my uncle's church, like going to a rock concert!

While I'd go to three churches every Sunday, each service was different, and I enjoyed it. The Methodist church was more subdued, the Baptist church was more upbeat, and the sanctified church had electric energy. All day Sunday, I was worshiping at church. Between one of the churches serving food, or somebody having us over for lunch, there was always something to eat too!

Church was a big part of my life throughout childhood. On Wednesday we had choir rehearsal. I was in church plays, programs, whatever, and we cleaned up the church every Saturday in preparation for Sunday. Sometimes on Saturday, with nobody supervising us, I'd get up in the front of the sanctuary and pretend I was giving a sermon. That's the closest I came to being a minister.

The logo of the local community center where I spent so much time as a kid was designed by my cousin. Written on part of that logo were the words "God, others and self." Those three words were supposed to be our universe. The kids in our program talked about that concept all the time, and I have carried that philosophy through challenges I have faced. When I was in a meeting with someone that wasn't going well, I'd think about that image—God, others, and self. It calmed me internally, and would help me get through the day.

One of the reasons why I chose Northwestern was because the school was founded by the Methodist ministry. I would visit the seminary frequently on campus. I'd walk there almost every day, because it was right in the middle of campus. It seems I was always passing the seminary on my way to other parts of the campus. I never applied to study there, but between Northwestern and seminaries in Chicago, I would've had a lot of choices had I decided to go in that direction. Instead, I chose pro football.

My family, despite its problems, prayed a lot when I was growing up. We prayed before meals. We prayed when times were tough. It's just something we did in our family. My father would lead the prayer at times, and my mother would, too. We had two tables, one in the kitchen and one in the dining room, because there were so many of us. But we always took time for prayer.

I also belonged to a community youth program sponsored by the Baptist church, spending almost all of my free time there. They had a gymnasium, swimming pool, and a game room where you could play cards. On Friday night they had free movies. You had to be ten years old to get a card to use the community center and as soon as I was old enough I was there. When you turned thirteen, you could come in at night by yourself.

Every summer, from the time I was ten through sixteen, I went to camps that the church held. As I got older I became a camp counselor. I learned first aid. We had swimming, boating, hiking. We'd identify trees and listen to bird calls. I used to be pretty good at identifying birds, and I still keep a birdhouse in the backyard of my house.

At night we'd lie on our backs, look at the stars, and talk about what it meant to be a part of this big universe that God created, and that we were just a small part of it.

Those church camps left a deep, deep impression on me. The kids who attended those camps weren't just from Hammond, but from East Chicago, Gary, and from places even further away. We had one kid from Ohio who came for the whole summer, staying with relatives in the area. Each cabin would hold six or seven of us.

I was there for three or four weeks every summer. And every night we'd have Bible sessions. It wasn't heavy-duty Bible study, but we'd talk about what went on that day and discuss philosophical questions. Did we make any contribution to society that day? Were we living the way Christ expected us to live? What could we do to make life better? We'd pray before every meal, and pray at night before we went to bed.

As kids, we'd come up with all kind of comments. Not all of the kids had religious faith. Some were really at camp just because their parents wanted to get rid of them for four weeks.

However, the lessons I learned at camp are still part of me today. And my religious faith is still at the forefront of my thoughts. When I meet a person for the first time, I like to give them faithful inspiration. I did that with Clifton Brown, who helped me write this book. I shook hands with him in my hotel room in Philadelphia, and gave him a poem that I keep on a card in my wallet, called "As a Man Thinks."

As a Man Thinks

Today I will think like a dynamic servant of God, because I am what I think.

I am not always what I think I am, but I am what I think.

I am not what I eat: I am what I think.

Clothes do not make the man, thinking makes the man.

Therefore I will keep my thought processes active and open to the voice of God.

God did not call me to a life of failure, but to a life of success. This being so, I cannot fail as long as I do His will, allowing him to work in and through me, motivating my every thought.

Because my God is a big God, I will think big with confidence, knowing my thoughts can never be bigger than my God.

Today I will think like the apostle Paul when he said, "I can do all things through Christ who strengthens me."

—Philippians 4:13

God has a plan for all of us, but it's very important how you spend the time that God has given you.

Part of God's plan for me was to play in the NFL. And my faith in God absolutely gave me courage on the football field.

When I stepped between those lines, I always felt that whatever happened was God's will. Whatever happened was meant to happen. It's kind of hard to explain, but that's honestly how I felt. Before every game, at both Northwestern and in the NFL, we'd pray in the locker room, we'd pray on the sidelines, and we'd pray on the field. There were times I'd pray during the course of a game, not for myself to do well, but for all of us to get out healthy.

But I was never terribly concerned about my physical well-being. I always felt if I hit the other guy harder than he hit me, that my opponent would absorb the most punishment. That's why I was hurt all the time. I kept coming after people. I wouldn't back down.

Nothing is more fulfilling to me than helping people who really need it. During my life I've worked as a board member, as a volunteer, and as an executive director with people who were homeless or who had drug and alcohol issues. You walk down the street of any city today, and you'll see people who may not look that bad, but who haven't had a home for a long period of time. You'd be surprised to know how many people are in that situation.

Our mission as people should be to reach out and help. I used to have a bad attitude about helping when I was a teenager. A minister who was with a youth program I was associated with said, "Only help those who want to help themselves." He meant that if somebody comes asking for something, and they're not willing to put their own energy into it, forget about them.

I felt that way for a long time, until I met this homeless guy named John in St. Cloud, Minn., when I was a local director of Big Brothers and Big Sisters. I used to grab a sandwich for lunch at a nearby place and I would pass by John who was sitting on a bench. When I first introduced myself to John and asked what his name was, he said, "Why, are you a cop?" I said, "No, I just see you a lot and figured I'd introduce myself so we could get to know each other."

The first time I bought him lunch I made the mistake of not asking him what he wanted. I got him a sub sandwich, but he couldn't eat it because his upper four teeth were missing. He couldn't chew down on the sandwich. So I went and got some soup for him. Every afternoon that he was there, I'd get a sandwich, he'd have soup, and we'd talk.

He had an amazing story. He was from St. Cloud, and as a young kid he never got his life together and had some problems with drugs. His father kicked him out of the house when he was a teenager. Some guy picked him up and raped him. Eventually he made his way back to St. Cloud, and he would sleep on the street. In the winter he'd sleep on the heat grates, during the summer he'd sleep under the overpass.

We convinced him to go to social services. After I left Big Brothers, I'd get an email every once in a while that he had stopped by to say hello. I think he believed that I wanted to help him. I don't beat people over the head with a sledgehammer. I just try to be the person God wants me to be and live that life, and people react to what they see.

Some people, like John, can't help themselves from where they started. Somebody has to be there to get them off the mat, to get them started, to care about them, to let them know that they're worth something, that God loves them. Those are people I pray for.

When I got to the Eagles, one of teammates, Maxie Baughan, was the team chapel leader. I joined him in that role, and we'd call ministers when we got to different cities, and they would come in and lead the chapel service.

"Whatever Irv and I needed to do, we'd find a preacher before a game," Baughan said. "With the Eagles and with the Rams, we'd never take the field without having some kind of chapel service."

I made a recommitment to my faith in the late sixties when I was playing for the Los Angeles Rams, while my first wife and our two children remained in Philadelphia. I was around a lot of Hollywood and entertainment people, thinking about things I had no business thinking about. My character was being tested. I owe a debt of gratitude to Dr. Ira Eshelman, a Presbyterian pastor and chaplain for NFL athletes, for getting me back on track with my faith. I have been on the right path ever since, despite life's challenges.

I'm always looking for new ways that my faith can play a significant role in the lives of others. A few years ago I became involved in a program called Love, Inc., which stood for "Love in the Name of Christ." I served as the executive director of Northwest Ramsey County, Minnesota.

Love, Inc. brought different churches together, networking to help people in need. One church may have provided clothes, another may have provided furniture, another may have assisted with helping someone find a job. But the idea was to assist more people through a network of churches, using the strengths of those churches to address a variety of needs.

Many of the churches we worked with around the country had trouble getting funding. But I still had some powerful experiences being involved with that organization. When I was chief executive officer of Big Brothers and Big Sisters of Central Minnesota, it was rewarding. But I was in more of a board, fundraising, organizational role. The most fun I had with Big Brothers and Big Sisters was playing with the little brother assigned to me, who was ten years old when I was seventy. Man, did he wear me out! But that was the same age I was when I lost my mother. It reminded me how important it was for this kid to have somebody to mentor him.

My role with Love, Inc. was very hands on, which is why I enjoyed it. I had to be in touch with the ministers and sit down with them. I had to visit the churches. I had to see what kind of programs we were running in person. I was deeply involved, and when people walked through the door, it was exciting to see them being helped before your eyes. We were getting immediate help to people and getting them back on their feet. I felt I was doing something to fulfill my role as a man of faith, and those are the kinds of situations I love.

There hasn't been one problem I've ever had that wasn't addressed in the Bible. To me, to solve any issue, you turn to Jesus Christ. I don't know of any issue of any kind on this planet that can't be solved that way.

When I was a kid in Hammond, I believed God was watching over me. It was true when I was doing the *NFL Today*, and it's true now. My faith is the thing that gets me through whatever I'm dealing with. Good times and bad times, it's always there.

As I've reached the age of seventy-seven, God has been with me every step of the way. I don't know how much longer my journey will last, but there's peace and comfort, knowing He will never leave me. When people ask why I seem genuinely happy, why I face each day with a smile, there's your answer.

6

HIGH SCHOOL FOOTBALL AND THE CHRIS-CROSS BACKFIELD

BEFORE there was a hip-hop duo named Kris Kross, there was the Chris-Cross backfield at Hammond High.

We were the original Chris-Cross, the starting backfield of Irv Cross and Christ Voris for the 1957 Hammond Wildcats. We made quite a name for ourselves as high school seniors, and the Chris-Cross nickname was part of our mystique.

By the time I reached high school, my ability to play football was starting to get me noticed. In fact, I was regarded as one of the top high school prospects in Northern Indiana. I had honed my skills playing a lot of sandlot football in Hammond. Maywood Park was kind of like the dividing line in my neighborhood. On the East side of Maywood Park was where the black families lived. On the other side were the middle- to upper-income families. But we all went to the same school, Maywood Elementary. In the fall we'd have pickup football games. I liked it, and it was fun to be with the guys. In a small town, the word gets around quickly. So people started talking about me, saying this kid who plays over at Maywood Park is pretty good, he's got some speed. He might be a good player at the high school one day.

To me, the most important thing about playing football was that it represented my free ticket to college. There was no way my father could afford to send me to college, nor did he have any interest in sending me. However, with my love for reading, and the academic confidence instilled in me by Miss Ewing, I believed I could graduate from college if given the opportunity. Playing football was going to open that door.

Hammond High and Hammond Tech were the two high schools in town. Hammond Tech was a vocational high school where kids learned trade skills. Almost all the black kids in town went to Hammond Tech, because they could get a job right out of high school. The steel mills in the area helped support many of the programs at Hammond Tech, and kids would graduate ready to work, and plenty of jobs were available at the machine shops, print shops, or steel mills.

My father didn't understand why I wanted to attend Hammond High instead of Hammond Tech. "What are you worried about going to college for?" my father asked. "Graduate from high school, get a job, or go into the service." For my father, the importance of a college degree was not even part of his thought process. The sooner I could put food on the table for myself and my family, the better.

Considering our family's economic situation, I understood why my father thought Hammond Tech was a better choice for me than Hammond High. But if I was going to attend college, I needed to take college prep courses. So Hammond High was where I went.

The school had about two thousand kids and, from what I remember, I was one of about six black kids in the entire high school. Hammond High was strong in sciences and mathematics, which prepared me well for Northwestern. But in almost all of my classes, I was the only black student. I guess that prepared me well for Northwestern, and for other things too!

Of course, Hammond was not immune to racism. When I was growing up in Hammond there were certain restaurants black people couldn't go to. When you went to the movies you sat in the balcony. One day when I was a young teenager, I was walking down the street with a white female counselor from the summer camp I attended. It was like four in the afternoon, broad daylight. This car passes by, and out the window this guy yells "Nigger lover." She turned to me and said, "What a bunch of jerks." I have to admit that it hurt me a bit, because they didn't know me from Adam, and they didn't know her either. Yet when they saw a white girl with a black kid walking down the street, they reacted that way. Just another reminder of the times we were in.

You can't make judgments about people solely based on how they look. And that's still a problem in our society today. If you're willing to look beyond what a person looks like, and get to know them, it's amazing the relationships you can build.

In many ways, I think growing up around different ethnic groups and religions prepared me well for life. When I was the only black person in a room, it was never uncomfortable or intimidating, nor did it make me behave differently. If there was discomfort in the room, it was coming from elsewhere and not from me. Others may try to put limitations on you, because of your race, your gender, or your background. But by the time

I was finished with Miss Ewing's fifth grade class, I never put limitations on myself. I had the mental freedom to chase my dreams.

Despite the paltry numbers of black students at Hammond High, nobody messed with me. I was a good athlete, strong, and of course I had plenty of brothers back home. The word was already out around Hammond—don't mess with the Cross kids. There's a whole bunch of them.

"Growing up in Hammond, with a big brother like Irv, was great for me," said Ray Cross. "You know that expression— it takes a village to raise a child. That's what Hammond was like. You could go to your neighbor's house and eat dinner. Nobody in our house had a door key. All those kids in the house, and nobody had a key. You didn't need one. We never locked the door.

"We didn't have the violence you see now. We didn't even have the racial strife, not like you see today. Our neighborhood wasn't just black. It was also a mixture of European and Hispanic. Black people had hope. We had our own taverns, our own hardware store, a black doctor was right in the neighborhood. We had a 10-block radius where you could find whatever you needed. I would trade today, for those days, in a heartbeat."

Since nobody bothered me, I didn't have any serious problems at Hammond High. In fact I have happy memories of my times there. Disliking somebody because of the color of their skin, or their religion, has just never been part of my makeup. I couldn't imagine being cruel to someone, or denying someone an opportunity, when I didn't even know them.

I played a number of sports at Hammond High—football, basketball, and running track. That's what boys in my day did, play sports. We didn't play video games and hang out at the mall. Sports were our recreation.

It was a long time before my father even knew that I had athletic talent. I remember when somebody finally told him, I was in high school. He was like, "Irv's doing what on the field? You say he's pretty good? Well how about that?" It was a pleasant surprise to him.

When I was sixteen, the Chicago White Sox were interested in signing me to a baseball contract. I had gone to a tryout and had done pretty well. But I wasn't interested. I wanted to go to college. I didn't want to go off to some minor league place, far away. I liked football better, and I also liked running track, where I was a hurdler and a sprinter.

However, football was my best sport. I played for a coach who became a legend in Northern Indiana. His name was Bernie Krueger. The football field at Hammond High is named after coach Krueger and for good reason. He won two state championship and 111 games during his eighteen-year tenure. We didn't win the state championship when I was there, but the teams I was part of built the momentum for his best seasons to come. Coach Krueger's teams had even more success after I graduated in 1957. From 1958–64, his teams went 53–7, including a 19-game winning streak.

Coach Krueger is one of the reasons I thought I wanted to become a coach. I was blessed to have many great coaches, and that's important for young people involved in athletics. Coaches play a valuable role in building young people if they do it the right way. As a coach, you teach players how to work together, how to handle success and failure, how to follow instructions, and how to earn what you get. All of that builds character.

Anybody who grew up in Hammond over the last fifty years knows coach Krueger. He graduated from Hammond High in 1944, served in the Navy, and was a heck of a college football player himself. He was an all Big Ten quarterback at the University of Illinois, and played on the winning Illinois Rose Bowl team in 1947. Sadly, coach passed away in 2016, but he lived to be ninety years old, and just like Miss Ewing, he touched plenty of lives.

I liked coach Krueger because he got his point across without doing a lot of screaming, and he really understood the game. And of course, I liked him because he trusted me with playing time. He had some nice things to say about me in the *Times of Northwest Indiana* after I won the Pete Rozelle Radio Television Award in 2009.

"I couldn't be happier for Irv," coach Krueger said. "He was a tremendous football player for me. I used him as a right halfback and he was good, but he was an even better defensive player. He proved that in the NFL."

I liked playing both offense and defense because you got to stay in the game. And playing both ways I believe makes you a better football player. I understand why playing both ways became obsolete, it's just too physically demanding in the modern era. However, what better way to understand offense than to play offense? There's no question that when I played cornerback exclusively in the NFL, my experience playing offense in high school and in college made me a better defensive back, and helped me diagnose plays faster.

Despite the racial dynamic at Hammond High, I made friends pretty easily. One of those friends was Christ Voris, who I always called "Chris." The Voris family lived on the other side of town, and white kids and black kids weren't always best friends in those days. But right off the bat, Chris and I became close. We were both good athletes, and very competitive.

Actually, I think Chris was more competitive than I was. When I saw the movie *Brian's Song* in 1971, which described the relationship between Gale Sayers and Brian Piccolo of the Chicago Bears, it brought back memories of me and Chris. Not only did we play football together, but we'd spend our summers working out together. Chris pushed me to go harder. If we agreed to do 100 pushups, Chris would keep going until we did 125. He always wanted one more wind sprint, one more drill, or fifteen more minutes working out. He was a fitness nut.

When we were seniors, Chris and I both played halfback and were tough to stop. I was faster and bigger than Chris, but he was a terrific player, a devastating blocker as a running back and a terrific hitter as linebacker.

Both Chris and I were voted All-State our senior season and he got a scholarship to Western New Mexico University. I would have loved to play college football with Chris, but he just wasn't a big enough guy to attract attention from the larger football schools.

When I was voted the Hammond High "Athlete of the Year" by the local newspaper, I felt that I was sharing that award with Chris and everybody else on the team. One of the great things about playing sports is the bonds and friendships you make with teammates. Chris became a friend for life.

After college, Chris actually played a year in the Canadian Football League, and had a great career as a high school teacher in California, coaching both football and wrestling. Just like I was voted into the Hammond High Hall of Fame in 1987, Chris was inducted posthumously in 2005.

Chris passed away in 2004, and his obituary mentioned that I was his best friend in high school. I was honored and deeply touched by that. Chris became a school teacher for more than thirty-five years and left a deep impression on many of his students. But Chris also left a deep mark on me. He was a truly good person, one who reaffirmed my belief that the things inside a person count more than what's on the outside.

Football brought Chris and I together. Mutual respect made our friendship last a lifetime. It didn't matter to us that we were from different races, from different sides of town. We had the same values and dreams, and we were willing to work hard for them.

There were other people in Hammond who assisted me, like Judge William Murray, who was a federal court judge. I cut his grass and took care of his yard so I could make extra money. He had a big house, a cook, and a housekeeper. While I was over there working, she'd cook me a huge meal. He liked me and was just trying to look after me. When he was home, he'd talk to me about things and try and keep me headed in the right direction. He couldn't understand all the things that black people had to go through to get ahead. But he clearly wanted me to succeed, and he thought I had potential.

HIGH SCHOOL FOOTBALL AND THE CHRIS-CROSS BACKFIELD

After high school, I was ready to leave Hammond and take my football career and education to the next level. But being part of the Chris-Cross backfield was a special time I will always treasure.

7

CHOOSING NORTHWESTERN

I**LOVE** Hammond and always will. But no matter where you are from, there are certain instances where you are reminded that race matters, no matter what you accomplish. As an example, after I won the Male Athlete of the Year Award, a couple of teammates took me to dinner to celebrate. The first restaurant we went to wouldn't let me in because I was black. The restaurant was right across the street from our high school.

Here I had just won a prestigious award in my hometown, but that didn't matter when it came to getting served in that restaurant. The answer was no. So of course, we found somewhere else to eat. But along with the happy thoughts of that evening, not being able to eat there is something that still sticks in my mind.

Nevertheless, I had too much positive energy to let anything deter me. Plenty of colleges had already let me know that if I wanted a full ride, I just had to say "Yes."

One of those schools was Northwestern. They had been tracking me for a few years, thanks in part to a person who became a good friend, Ed Vennon.

Ed was a Hammond High graduate who was a couple of years older than me. He was already at Northwestern as a student, and he had become a volunteer recruiter for the university. Ed loved Northwestern and, of course, he wanted me to go there.

In 1957, this country was still a very tough place to live for blacks. Ed spent an untold amount of time with me at my home, and drove me to Evanston for my meeting with legendary coach Ara Parseghian. My decision to attend Northwestern was made so much easier because Ed was there.

"I was involved with recruiting at Northwestern from an early age," said Ed Vennon. "My father was a high school official for football, basketball, and a little baseball. He got tied to Northwestern through a colleague at work and started birddogging some athletes for them.

"I first met Irv when he was a freshman and I was a senior in high school. There weren't many black students at our high school at all. The ones who were there, at least the boys, were usually athletes. Irv played football, basketball, and ran track.

"My first memory of him was in the gym after school. A bunch of loud guys came into the gym showing up for freshman basketball practice. It struck me right then and there that Irv Cross was the leader of the group. I don't know why. There was something about his demeanor. It was something about the rest of the kids, and the way they seemed to admire him. But that caught my eye, and I started to follow his career more closely.

"After I left high school and went to Northwestern, I'd talk to the coaches at Hammond about Irv. I always got glowing reports about what a great teammate he was, and what a leader he was."

That's the same impression I had of him.

"When the newspaper published the story about Irv winning Athlete of the Year, they used a picture of Irv in the kitchen fixing food for his siblings. That's an unusual portrait for an athlete getting a prestigious award. But that gives you an idea of the kind of responsibilities Irv had.

"I've been told that when Irv didn't show up for school, it was understood he was home taking care of some of his siblings. The school understood that, and Irv didn't get in trouble for it.

"What school wouldn't want a young man who was a great athlete, a humble guy, and who also took care of his family? I thought he'd be great for Northwestern."

I was impressed that Northwestern followed the rules when they recruited me. Other schools were willing to cheat.

One school, I won't say which one, said they would give me a full ride, $500 spending money, and a brand new 1957 Ford Fairlane convertible if I came. This guy from the school pulled the Fairlane up to the front of our house and parked it. My father was there and saw the whole thing.

This guy gives the keys to me, and I'm staring at the car. Boy, did it look good!

But when he left, neither my dad nor I thought it was right. We didn't know the first thing about NCAA rules, but a new car, and $500 a month? It just didn't feel right to us. Five hundred dollars a month was more than my father was making! They also gave me a contact name to call for anything I needed once I got to campus.

A couple of days later, coach Parseghian called from Northwestern. He said, "We can't offer you anything except a first-class education, and an opportunity to play in the Big Ten."

That was good enough for me. I had already taken my visit to Northwestern and loved it. I was impressed with everyone in the athletic department.

I told Parseghian, "Coach, I'm on my way."

The only thing I didn't like about Northwestern was the cold weather. I was used to the climate growing up not that far away in Hammond. But the campus was right along the lake. You had to know the best way to avoid that heavy, freezing wind coming off the lake when you walked across campus. There were days when it would be blowing 30 or 40 miles per hour. It felt like it was going to knock you down. When you got inside a building, you'd stay inside as long as possible before you went to the next one. I'd just go into the library and stay for hours. The library was right in the middle of campus, so that was nice.

Northwestern was a serious environment for learning. Some people knew I was an athlete, but nobody made a big deal about it, especially my professors. That's the way I liked it. Everything was secondary to academics. I won some academic awards while I was there, and graduated in the top six percent of my class.

"Irv was always about business, not horseplay," Ray said. "That led to his academic excellence. A lot of people assumed that when he went to Northwestern, it was on just an athletic scholarship. Not true. It was half athletic, half academic, and he graduated at age 21 while still playing football. That's not easy to do."

I had four wonderful years at Northwestern and loved the experience, both on and off the field. It was far enough away from Hammond to be on my own, but close enough where I could get home quickly.

I was the captain of both the football and the track teams, and I also got to play for coach Parseghian, who went on to become a legendary figure at Notre Dame a few years later. Parseghian took over a Northwestern program that had been in shambles. In 1955, the year before he arrived, Northwestern went 0–8–1, including an embarrassing 49–0 loss to Ohio St. There was even talk about the program leaving the Big Ten.

The grumbling about Parseghian continued during my freshman year in 1957, when the team went winless at 0–9. But in 1958 we were 5–4, in 1959 we were 6–3, and in 1960 we were 5–4. That may not look that impressive on paper, but considering where the program had been, and considering the competition we played against, those were major accomplishments.

If that 1958 Northwestern team had suffered a losing year, who knows if the school would have stuck with Parseghian. But we delivered for him. We blew out Michigan, 55–24, to let people know we were for real. We led the Wolverines, 43–0, at halftime, and I've heard that when the halftime score went over the Associated Press wire, a lot of newspapers thought it was a typo!

Our biggest win was a 45–13 blowout of Oklahoma and their legendary coach, Bud Wilkinson. The Sooners had won 107 of the previous 117 games. But fate was on our side. Rain turned our home field into a muddy mess, and the Sooners fumbled 11 times! That victory gave Parseghian and our program more national attention, and set the stage for better things to come.

There's something else pretty cool about my time at Northwestern. Somebody there at the same time would later become my co-worker. His name was Brent Musberger.

"Northwestern is a great school, and it was great for both me and Irv," Musberger said. "One important thing was the school's proximity to the Windy City. In our era, when you came out of Northwestern, you were able to get jobs. Chicago was a great spot for jobs, even better than New York.

"I certainly was not an outstanding student. But I enjoyed the environment. It was a great people place and continues to be. I'm still in contact with so many Northwestern people. Northwestern helped put me into broadcasting. Bob Wussler (creator of the *NFL Today*) brought me from Chicago to New York, and the rest is history. A headmaster of mine at a private school put the idea of attending Northwestern into my head. He told me, 'You like sports, you like journalism. Go there.' That was a great piece of advice.

"Those Northwestern teams that Irv played on were critical to Parseghian's career, especially after the 0–9 season. Parseghian was losing games with guys like Bo Schembechler on his coaching staff. People were starting to wonder about Ara. Who's this dude who had come in to coach from Miami [Ohio]? Could he get the job done?

"When Irv and his class joined the varsity in 1958, it wasn't long before Northwestern was stalking the very top of the Big Ten, capable of playing with anybody. They had some shocking wins over Ohio St. and Notre Dame. And those Northwestern teams Irv played on had talent. Irv, Ron Burton, the Kimbrough brothers (Albert and Elbert), and Fred Williamson were some of the stars on those teams. They set the table for Parseghian to leave Northwestern after the 1963 season to become Notre Dame's head coach. The rest, as they say, is history, and Parseghian proved to be an all-time great."

Parseghian instilled in us that we could beat anyone. As he once said, "A good coach will make his players see what they can be rather than what they are."

Another favorite Parseghian quote of mine is, "You know what it takes to win. Just look at my fist, it's strong and you can't tear it apart. As long as there's unity, there's strength. We must become so close with the bonds of loyalty and sacrifice, so deep with the conviction of the sole purpose, that no one, no group, no thing, can ever tear us apart."

One of the highlights of my college football career at Northwestern was a 30–24 victory over Notre Dame in my junior year. Playing wide receiver, I caught a 78-yard touchdown pass from John Talley, which at the time was the longest touchdown reception in Northwestern history.[1]

In those days, freshmen didn't play varsity football. So when I joined the Northwestern varsity as a sophomore, I played both wide receiver, defensive back and even some defensive end at 190 pounds. We didn't have much depth, but Parseghian was great at moving guys around and getting the most out of them. I really didn't care what position I played, as long as I got a chance to play.

I loved the attitude of those Northwestern teams. No matter how big the school, we never backed down.

The Kimbroughs, Albert and Elbert, and Mike Stock and Dick Thornton and the others in our freshman class of 1957 were all from winning high school backgrounds. If you had suggested to Elbert Kimbrough we might lose our opener in 1959 to Oklahoma or to Notre Dame, he'd punch your lights out.

* * *

Parseghian was a great coach, terrific motivator, and an amazing teacher. I loved playing for him and learned a lot. His teams at Northwestern beat Notre Dame three straight times from 1959–61, and there was no doubt those victories helped Parseghian eventually get the head coaching job in South Bend. The Irish figured if Parseghian could beat Notre Dame with Northwestern's players, he could definitely win games with Notre Dame's talent. We'd always get a few injuries at the start of the season, which made it difficult to win late in the season when we had to go with some of our backups.

But we had some good talent—including three guys who made it to the NFL—me, Fred "The Hammer" Williamson, and Ron Burton, who was a close friend of mine. We were among the first black players at Northwestern, and I'm sure we helped pave the way for guys who followed.

Ron became a role model for me, a year older than me, a teammate, and a great player. We had a lot in common. Ron's mother had also died when he was young. He was a devout Christian like myself, and he also didn't drink.

As a great running back, Ron led us to a 6–0 start in 1960 before we faded late in the season. Ron set school records at the time for most career points (130) and touchdowns (21), and it was clear Ron had the talent to play pro football. He was the ninth overall pick by the Eagles in the 1960 draft, and the first draft pick ever by the Boston Patriots in the 1960 AFL draft.

Ron may have played for the Eagles just like me, but his religion led him to the Patriots. In those days the AFL played on Friday or Saturday, while the NFL played on Sunday. Ron didn't want to play on Sundays because he wanted to worship. He told me that led to his decision to sign with the Patriots.

Ron built a great life for himself in New England both on and off the field for his wife and five children. All of Ron's children eventually went to Northwestern, which shows you the kind of impact the school had on him. In 1985, he started the Ron Burton Training Village in rural Massachusetts, which is a summer camp for underprivileged kids.

The work of Ron's camp has continued, although he passed away in 2003. The Patriots' community service award is named after Ron, and the most recent winner was star tight end Rob Gronkowski, who would have made Ron proud with his remarks.

"This award is an honor, and it's so appreciated," Gronkowski said during an interview on Patriots.com. "To accept it on behalf of the Burton family, their name, and accepting it from the Kraft family, Mr. Kraft directly, is just an honor . . . I just want to put this trophy out in front of all my other trophies I got on the trophy case. That's how much it means."

I miss Ron as a friend, but I'm proud that he was another example of the kind of people that Northwestern has produced.

Before I graduated from Northwestern in 1961, I was fortunate enough to be named the school's male athlete of the year for accomplishments in football and track. I was truly humbled by that, and a little embarrassed to be singled out. When they gave me the award, I told the school I didn't want to accept it, but I have it at home somewhere. Don't get me wrong, the award means a lot to me. It's just that I'm very reluctant to accept individual praise.

I had some memorable experiences at Northwestern as I was truly becoming a man, on my own for the first time in life. I also learned a valuable lesson about stereotyping.

It was my freshman year, and it must have been orientation week because school hadn't started yet. The professor was conducting one of those orientation exercises where everyone was introducing themselves, telling each other where we came from.

I'm sitting next to an Asian student. He hadn't done his presentation yet. I said to him, "Why don't you tell us about Japan?" He said, "I don't know anything about Japan. I'm from California."

I felt the embarrassment come over me. I thought to myself, "Irv, you jerk." If I could have crawled into a hole, I would've done it.

All my life when something like that was done to me, when people made assumptions based on what I looked like, I resented it. Then I turned around and did the same darn thing. I apologized to him later. I told him I was sorry, really sorry.

He said, "That's OK. I get that a lot."

But I never forgot.

Meanwhile, Northwestern presented challenges both academically and socially. Northwestern is on the quarter system instead of the semester system. We'd do a semester's work in what seemed like almost half the time. I screwed up my freshman year, and didn't plan the first quarter very well. I thought I could walk in, take the exams, and be okay. To my shock, I ended up with two Cs and two Ds the first quarter! I had never gotten grades like that before in my life! I was on academic probation! I was mortified.

That's when my library routine picked up dramatically. I was in classes Monday, Wednesday, and Friday, but I learned I had to study hard on my off days as well. I had to plan my time much better than I'd been doing.

Fortunately, I made the adjustment and started getting the kind of grades I had grown accustomed to. By the first quarter of my senior year, I already had enough credits to graduate. So I started to take other courses just to see what they were like.

One course I took was constitutional law. Boy was I humbled. Just about everybody in that course was planning to become a lawyer except me. The professor was a taskmaster, and he loved to call on students to make arguments during class. Getting out of that class was a real battle. For his final, not only did you have a written exam, but you had to see the professor and argue against him about a legal matter for an hour.

Now I can talk to college students about the adjustment from high school to college, and how you can't allow yourself to get too discouraged early. For most students, if you hang tough your freshman year, things will get better.

Northwestern was the place where I had my first and only drink of alcohol. During my freshman year, I went with some teammates to a jazz club in Chicago. The guys were drinking beer, and one of my teammates, Willie Jones, ordered one for me. I took one sip and didn't like it. If I had sipped the whole beer, maybe I would have acquired a taste for it. But I never did.

That's the extent of my experience with drinking. I didn't like the taste, but it was more mental for me than physical. It was my father's drinking problem that was on my mind. I had sworn I would never use alcohol, or smoke cigarettes, and that one beer was my first and last drink.

A gentleman by the name of Charles "Doc" Glass was also extremely important to me during my time at Northwestern. There weren't many black students on campus, which made social life for us a bit difficult. If I remember correctly, there were only about 12 black students at the time. Doc and his wife, Helen, used to invite black students to their house regularly as a place where we could hang out, play cards, and listen to music in a comfortable environment. It gave us a place to unwind, to be around each other, and help cope with the pressures we all felt as students. Doc is now deceased, but I owe a lot to him and his family.

The summer of my sophomore year, Ed Vennon's father got me a summer job at a steel company in Gary, Indiana, but I didn't have a way to get from Hammond to Gary without my own transportation. I needed to stay on campus for the summer and land a job near Northwestern.

When coach Parseghian found out, he got me a summer job on campus with the building and grounds crew—but I still needed a place to stay. Ed was a member of a fraternity and was the summer manager of the frat house. Not surprisingly, there was one potential problem: There were no black members in his fraternity.

Since Ed was the house manager, he told his fraternity that I was staying in the frat house for the summer—period. I paid him five bucks a week for rent.

"It took Irv about two days to charm everybody in the fraternity house," Vennon said. "If you know the man, it's not surprising.

"What a career he had at Northwestern. He was junior men's honorary, senior men's honorary, co-captain two years of the football team, and captain at least one year of the track team.

"Considering the social situation for blacks at Northwestern during those times, I suspect there were times it had to be harder for him than he let on. If he wanted, I think Irv Cross could've been an actor. I think there were times he couldn't have been as comfortable as he seemed to be, but it never showed.

"The guy's amazing. He's outgoing, affable, very bright, very loyal, very trustworthy. It's almost impossible not to like Irv."

I feel the same way about Ed. He's a great friend, a man of high character, a fighter for the less fortunate. He never says a word about his own obstacles, and loves Northwestern. Ed was stricken with polio as a child and could not run or jump, but I felt his presence with every step I took on and off the field. Ed told me to follow him to Northwestern, and I'm glad I did. When I left, I was prepared for the next chapter in my life.

8

THE DRAFT

AFTER my football career at Northwestern, I wasn't sure if I was good enough to play in the NFL. Things weren't like they are today, with prospects being evaluated and compared to each other for months on end. The NFL combine didn't exist. There was no Mel Kiper Jr. on television, producing mock drafts and predicting which players would go to which teams.

I wanted the Bears to draft me. That way I'd be close to home in Hammond, where my friends and family could see me play. Also, George Halas was the coach of the Bears, and he was a legend.

The 1961 NFL draft took place at the Warwick Hotel in Philadelphia and, when it started, I had no idea the Eagles would draft me. I wish I could tell you what I was doing on the day I was drafted, but I can't remember. I know I wasn't sitting around the house, waiting for the phone to ring. It wasn't the biggest day of my life. I wasn't going to walk across a stage and get a hug from the commissioner. I knew I wasn't going to be a first-round pick, and I knew I wasn't signing a multi-million dollar contract.

My rookie contract was for $10,000—a $1,500 signing bonus in advance, and $8,500 more the rest of the year if I made the team. My NFL salary peaked out at $60,000 when I got traded to the Rams. Today that's chump change. Remember, I made the Pro Bowl in back-to-back years (1964–65). If I was a Pro Bowl cornerback today, I could see myself holding out for more money!

We had a players' union back then, but it didn't really have much power. Guys rarely held out for more money, as the owners had all the leverage when it came to contracts. You also didn't have free agency. We had a saying back then: If you were a player rep for your team, don't buy a house. Player reps often got traded. We didn't have agents. You just got what you could.

With part of my signing bonus I bought a used car, a 1958 Pontiac Star Chief. The first car I ever had was a 1951 Chevrolet that one of my former teammates at Northwestern sold me for $25! I called the car "Rags," because the bottom of the car was starting to corrode, and you could see little holes at the bottom. But that thing was a tank. I never had any problems starting it. On those cold days when nobody else's car would start, mine would! I had Rags for part of a winter and spring quarter, and then I upgraded when I signed with the Eagles!

I also remember that Bucko Kilroy was the area scout for the Eagles, and he came to Northwestern to talk to me about a possible contract. He tried to track me down all day long, going from classroom to classroom. When we finally met, I told him I didn't think I could play for the Eagles because they played on Sunday, which was a day of worship. As you can imagine, Bucko wasn't too pleased to hear me say that, especially since I wasn't a hot-shot first-round pick like Ron Burton!

I had mixed emotions about playing on Sundays if I were to join an NFL team. From that standpoint, playing in the AFL seemed more appealing, because their games were on Fridays and Saturdays. However, I didn't want to eliminate the NFL as a possibility for me before the draft even took place. Ultimately, I decided that participating in chapel services before games was a compromise I could live with if I played in the NFL.

Plenty of big names went in the 1961 draft. You might remember a lot of them. Mike Ditka went to the Bears at No. 5, Tom Matte went No. 7 to the Colts, Billy Kilmer went No. 11 to the 49ers, Herb Adderly went No. 12 to the Packers, Bob Lilly went No. 13 to the Cowboys, and Fran Tarkenton went No. 29 to the Vikings.

In all, there were seven future Hall of Famers taken in the '61 draft: Adderly, Ditka, Lilly, Tarkenton, Deacon Jones, Billy Shaw, and Jimmy Johnson . . . and I don't mean the FOX analyst Jimmy Johnson, who coached the Cowboys to two Super Bowl championships. This Jimmy Johnson played cornerback like me, and he was a great one. Not only did Johnson have a brilliant career with the 49ers with 47 interceptions, but his brother Rafer Johnson was a former decathlete who won a gold medal in the 1960 Olympics. Talk about an athletic family!

There were 20 rounds in the 1961 draft, with 280 players selected. Imagine what it would be like today, watching a 20-round draft on television. I'm sure the networks would have a ball with that![2]

I wonder what the scouting report would have been on me, and how I would have fared at the combine? The scouting process was different back then, but here's one similarity between then and today: the draft was an imperfect science. Some guys who should have been picked much higher were overlooked, especially if they came from smaller schools. Like Deacon Jones, who wasn't drafted until the 14th round. Deacon Jones, a 14th round pick? Give me a break. I played with Deacon for three years (1966–68) when I was with the Rams, and he might be the greatest pass rusher who ever lived, probably the most dominant teammate I ever had. He is the man most responsible for popularizing the quarterback sack, and defensive ends owe him a debt of gratitude for popularizing the position.

Jones was the product of a historically black college (Mississippi Valley St.), and in 1960 not everyone in the NFL realized, or wanted to realize, that HBCU schools were such a gold mine for talent. In 1985, another legendary player came from Mississippi Valley St. and silenced any doubters he had—Jerry Rice. Think about that. A small HBCU school in Mississippi has produced the greatest pass rusher and the greatest wide receiver of all time. Not bad.

Deacon had a much harder path to the NFL than I did. He spent a year at South Carolina St., but had his scholarship revoked after he participated in a civil rights march. Then after going to Mississippi Valley St., he had to prove himself as a 14th-round pick.

Deacon got the last laugh though, winning the NFL Defensive Player of the Year twice, making the Pro Bowl eight times, and being inducted into the Pro Football Hall of Fame. Not only did Deacon scare quarterbacks to death, he could be scary as a teammate. If you messed up a play, Deacon would just stare at you in the huddle. You knew what it meant. Don't mess up again!

The best NFL team I ever played on was with Deacon—the 1967 Los Angeles Rams. We were 11–1–2, and during the regular season we beat the defending champion, the Green Bay Packers, and we ended the season on an eight-game winning streak.

I thought we were going to the Super Bowl. But in those days, the NFL had a ridiculous format where home-field advantage was determined on a round-robin basis, not by best record during the regular season. So even though we had a better record than the Packers (9–4–1), it was their division's turn to host a playoff game. So we traveled to Green Bay for the playoffs, actually to Milwaukee County Stadium, and lost 28–7. That set up the famous "Ice Bowl" game the following week between the Packers and Cowboys, which the Packers won on their way to another championship.

That playoff loss to the Packers was the most devastating defeat of my career. It still bothers me today. I knew my career was closer to the end, than the beginning, and I never got closer to winning a championship.

I had no idea that's how my NFL future would play out as I headed into the draft. This is what happened to me on draft day. The Eagles took me in the seventh round, the 98th pick overall. It was definitely a surprise. I had never even been to Philadelphia before, and knew nothing of the city.

Here's what I did know. The Eagles had just won the NFL championship in 1960. Which meant they had plenty of talented players, which also meant it wouldn't be easy to make the team.

The guy starting for the Eagles at right cornerback was Tom Brookshier, who would become not only a teammate, but a friend, and later a colleague as a broadcaster at CBS. "Brookie," as we called him, was a heck of a football player. There was no way I was taking the starting job at right corner from him, especially with the team coming off a championship season.

The Eagles viewed me as a player who could be groomed to take Brookie's place when he got older. But I wasn't convinced this Eagles thing would work out for me, and I did have other options. I was also drafted by the New York Titans of the American Football League.[3]

Knowing that two different organizations had drafted me helped build my confidence. It was an indication that scouts and coaches out there believed in my talent.

Just like Ron Burton, I was serious about not wanting to play on Sunday, and I was thinking about signing with the Titans. But when we were negotiating my contract, somebody with the Eagles came up with an idea.

"How would you feel if we had a chapel service or Bible study before the games, so that you could still worship on Sundays?" I was asked.

That sounded good to me, and one of the Eagles' young players, Maxie Baughan was already involved with organizing Bible study with the team. That made the idea of playing for the Eagles more appealing, so I signed.

Even though I never played in the AFL, I was a big fan of the league coming into existence. It opened up so many more opportunities for players. There was a heavy-duty war between the two leagues over players, which led to bigger contracts.

After signing with the Eagles, I was hungry but also realistic. In football, you're always one snap away from a potential career-ending injury. I was a good student in college, I had my degree from Northwestern, and I wasn't counting on a career in football to put a roof over my head.

When I see the kind of money that NFL players make today, I admit it makes you wonder sometimes what that must feel like. Especially since there are so many specialists now—nickel cornerbacks, third-down receivers, situational pass rushers. I never had to worry about the situation I was going to play. If the other team had the ball, I was playing!

If I didn't make the Eagles, my plan was to enroll in graduate school at Northwestern. When I reported for training camp, I even told the coach and general manager, "If you think you're going to cut me, cut me early. Then I can get back to Northwestern in time for the fall semester."

If I had gone undrafted, or if the Eagles had cut me, I doubt I would have ever played professional football. Once I started grad school, I would have finished and maybe gone into teaching, or coaching, or both.

But God had a different plan for me. Playing in the NFL opened doors that I never could have imagined. Like a career in broadcasting—the last thing on my mind when I entered the NFL.

In the sixties, NFL players thought differently than today's players. We had to work offseason jobs, because the money wasn't good enough to play football and do nothing else. But once the salaries exploded, players went to college thinking more about football and less about education.

For me, that was never the case. When I entered the NFL, I was still a student at heart—now I was just playing football for a living. That studious approach paid off, both on the field and off. When I first got to Philly, I had my doubts. But I was determined to show the Eagles they didn't make a mistake when they drafted me.

9

WELCOME TO THE NFL

MY first professional training camp with the Eagles was a rude awakening.

I didn't get much respect on Day 1, as a seventh-round draft pick joining a team that had won the NFL championship the year before. I wore jersey No. 32 in college, and I was kind of hoping to wear that in the NFL.

Forget about that. The Eagles' equipment guy was an older gentleman. He looked like he had been with the team longer than I had been alive. When I arrived at the equipment room, he just threw a jersey at me and said, "Here's your jersey. No. 27."

"How about No. 32?" I asked.

"No. 27," he said.

Training camp was intense. We practiced twice a day, in the morning and in the afternoon. When you practiced in the morning, your uniform would get soaking wet from perspiration. The vets would get their stuff washed between practices. But if you were a rookie, your stuff from the morning didn't get washed until the evening. So you'd put the same dirty stuff back on for the afternoon practice, still wet from the morning.

I don't think I uttered a word the first day of practice. I felt like I was a kid back in my house in Hammond, too shy to speak. I just wanted to do something to convince the coaches I had a chance to make the squad.

My shining moment came quickly. Our new starting quarterback was Sonny Jurgensen, whose golden right arm eventually took him to the Hall of Fame. Jurgensen figured he would test me, the fresh rookie cornerback from Northwestern. Early in practice, he sent Tommy McDonald to my side, and McDonald ran an out-and-up, hoping to beat me for a big play.

I ran with Tommy stride for stride and, when I turned, the ball was right there, and I made the interception. Not bad for my first time being targeted as a rookie.

Trying to defend NFL wide receivers was a huge step up from college, as I learned quickly. It's one thing to have speed, and I was pretty fast. But the great wide receivers have technique. They run routes smoothly, without revealing when they will change direction, change speed, or stop. The best NFL wide receivers set you up, and feast on your mistakes.

Cornerbacks live a lonely existence, out on the island covering guys one-on-one. You can't afford to relax or lose concentration, even for just a split second. If you do, it can be six points for the other team, followed by cuss words and angry looks from your teammates and coaches.

The Eagles had two excellent veteran wide receivers my rookie year—McDonald and Pete Retzlaff. For them, having a rookie cornerback to test made the practices a little more fun. For me, it was a crash course on playing cornerback in the NFL. Trying to defend McDonald and Retzlaff would've been tough under any circumstances, but Jurgensen was a dart thrower, one of the most accurate and purest passers the NFL has ever seen. I was fresh meat, and a few times they burned me like a log in a fireplace.

McDonald beat me five times in a row so easily it was ridiculous. It definitely discouraged me, and I thought about hanging up my cleats. I mean, if McDonald was schooling me with ease, what chance did I have? But Tom Brookshier talked to me, along with Pete Retzlaff and McDonald, who helped me tremendously.

With Jurgensen throwing to McDonald and Retzlaff, there was nowhere for me to hide during those first practices with the Eagles. But I was learning quickly. The veteran tricks that McDonald and Retzlaff showed me in training camp prepared me when I saw those same moves from opposing wide receivers.

The coaches eventually settled on putting me at right corner, my strongest side, playing behind Brookshier.

Fortunately for me, Brookshier believed in taking care of rookies. He was a mentor to me, both on and off the field. There was the typical rookie hazing at dinner, when the vets made the rookies stand up and sing their school fight song. I sang the Northwestern fight song with pride, so well that Jimmy Carr, one of my teammates, figured I deserved a hand.

"Let's hear it for Irv," Carr said, and the vets sang out,

Hooray for Irv

Hooray at last

Hooray for Irv

He's a horse's ass.

Everybody broke out laughing. but it was all in good fun. And the more guys needled me, I knew they saw me as a guy who would be part of the team.

Not every day was smooth. One time, Tommy put a head-and-shoulder fake on me, before cutting to the outside. By the time Sonny threw the ball, I was toast. I couldn't have caught Tommy with a bicycle.

One time, Pete had fun at my expense. The pattern he ran wasn't even that long, but it was precise. When Pete made his cut, he left me. Of course, Sonny's throw was right on the money, so Pete didn't have to break stride. He simply caught the ball, and turned toward the goal line with nothing but green grass between him and the end zone.

There were only 14 teams in the NFL in 1961, and 34 roster spots. That's a pretty small base of players, and once you had established yourself as a player in the league, it was almost like a big fraternity. It seemed like most of us knew each other. If I was in New York or Washington, I'd spend time with guys from other teams like Sam Huff and Y. A. Tittle.

The fraternity was even smaller for black players. You didn't have black quarterbacks. You didn't have black middle linebackers.

I went to a Big Ten school, but blacks from historically black colleges were still fighting that stigma around the NFL that the competition they played against wasn't as good. As I said before, it took guys like Deacon Jones and many others to change that perception.

We used to laugh about having four black guys on the Eagles in 1961 including myself.

They had four so they could pair us off as roommates. You couldn't have an odd number of black guys because one of us would be left not having a black roommate. So it was two, four, or six. That's another reason I was really thinking about grad school at the start of training camp. I didn't think the Eagles would keep five black guys, and that meant I could literally be the odd man out.

One of my black teammates on the Eagles was Timmy Brown. He was a good running back, and he went into show business. He wanted to be a singer, and he was serious about it.

My rookie year, we played the Steelers on the road. Timmy says to me, "Can you hang out in the lobby for a little while? I've got somebody coming over." I waited a few hours, but it was getting late. Coach [Skorich] saw me hanging down in the lobby and said, "What are you doing down here?" I told him I just couldn't sleep.

Finally I just had to go upstairs. I knocked on the door.

"What?" I heard Timmy say from inside.

"I've got to come in," I said.

"You can't come in!" Timmy yelled back.

So I went back to the lobby. Finally after a while, I went back upstairs. And guess who was coming out of our room? Diana Ross.

Timmy says, "Hey Di, this is Irv."

"Hi," I said, stars in my eyes, as he walked her downstairs.

Of course, I was an even bigger fan of Diana Ross and the Supremes after that.

I wasn't getting attention from Diana Ross like Timmy, but I figured out how to get the coach's attention. During one chalkboard session my rookie season, our defensive backfield coach

Jerry Williams gave out a test to see if we knew our assignments. It was pretty comprehensive. Everyone else finished their test, handed it to Jerry, and walked out the room. I was the last guy, busy writing away. Jerry said, "Irv, do you need any help?" I said, "No, I'll be finished shortly." When I finally gave him my paper, he looked down and said, "Holy smokes, what's this?" He wanted us to put down our individual defensive assignment. I had put down the assignments for all 11 defensive players.

I said, "Coach, that's how we did it at Northwestern."

So as a rookie, I became one of the Eagles' signal callers along with Tom Brookshier and Maxie Baughan. I'll never forget the first time I was calling the defense in a game, with Brookie and Maxie already out of the game. We're in the huddle, and I looked up across the huddle, and Chuck Bednarik is waiting for me to call the signal. Bednarik is a future Hall of Fame player, a legend, and quite intimidating. I'm thinking, *Chuck Bednarik is waiting for me to tell him what to do?* I almost couldn't get the words out, but I did.

Jerry was impressed. My play started to improve once I had the defense down cold. My teammates were able to help me more, because I understood my role within the defense and how my assignment fit into the scheme.

Jerry had a major influence on my career, both as a coach and a confidant. I told the

Spokesman-Review how much Jerry meant to me when he died in 1999.

Jerry was one of the brightest guys I ever met, and he taught me plenty about football. George Allen often talked about his own nickel defense, but the concept of the nickel defense originated with Jerry Williams. And he wasn't just an offensive or defensive expert. Jerry was a football expert. He used the run-and-shoot offense in Canada, and we used it sometimes during my first year in Philly.

I kept detailed notes on opponents throughout my nine-year career. I'd build a personal file on every wide receiver in the league. I'd write down their strengths, their weaknesses, and each year the file kept growing. It was like a security blanket. Every time I was matched up against Bob Hayes, or Paul Warfield, I had my notebook I could turn to for reference. Later when I worked at *NFL Today*, I built the same kind of notebook on players.

By the time I started playing preseason games as a rookie, my confidence was growing and my teammates and coaches started believing in me. They could see me blossoming, and I was earning the respect of the veteran players.

"You knew Irv Cross was always going to give you everything he's got and more," said Maxie Baughan. "He came to the Eagles the year after I did. After Tom Brookshier got hurt, he was the starting right corner and I was the starting right linebacker. We were together like that, both with the Eagles and with the Rams, and I knew I could trust him. But all this time, I didn't know Irv was one of fifteen kids. Wow! No wonder he played the way he did. He was used to fighting for a plate!

"Irv had a great attitude and a great approach to the game. He was always ready to go. I don't think I saw another player in my NFL career that was quite like Irv, because he didn't worry about anything. He always believed himself. He was a true football player, and a truer friend.

"Irv took up for me on many occasions. I was a hothead, and he was the calm one. One game against the Colts, I threw my helmet on the ground, and it must have bounced 10 or 15 yards into the air. I've got a picture of that helmet being thrown. Johnny Unitas, the rest of the Colts and the Eagles, were looking at each other wanting to fight. There was one man on that picture of 22 players who was looking up at the helmet. That man was Irv Cross. He caught my helmet like it was a basketball. He got it back to me because he didn't want to see me get thrown out of the game."

Getting immediate respect from a player like Maxie meant a lot to me. He was a big-time player who made nine Pro Bowls during his career. He started as a rookie with the Eagles in 1960 and became an integral part of their championship defense from Day 1. He will always be revered at Georgia Tech, where he won the SEC Player of the Year Award as a senior, playing both ways as a linebacker and center.

After a few weeks of camp and preseason games, I felt pretty certain I was going to make the team. Some guys had already been cut. Maybe they had talent, but they simply weren't tough enough. Training camp in the sixties was brutal. We had real two-a-day sessions in the heat. Not this walkthrough stuff they have today, sometimes with no pads. The hitting was vicious. Coaches wanted to weed out guys who wouldn't hit, especially in the secondary. I never had a problem with trying to tackle somebody, and that was one thing the coaches liked.

I did have another problem, though. It was the way I tackled. I often led with my head, which was a habit I couldn't break. I'd torpedo a guy down low when he was running, but my head was often the first thing that made contact with the ball carrier's legs.

"You see, in college, I was a [defensive] end," I explained in an article in the *Philadelphia Bulletin*. "We were taught to plant the head in the center of a man's body and slide off. That's been my ruination in pro ball, because these guys are so big, they're catching me with their kneecaps."

Going from college to the NFL, the collisions were more violent and the guys you were tackling knew how to protect their bodies. That's something I had to learn. It was a different game. I had to be smarter. I had to learn to keep my head out of the way.

Teams ran the ball more back then, and were committed to outside running plays like the power sweep. When I played corner against those sweeps, you had a guard or tackle coming at you, and if you managed to avoid that block, you still had to deal with power runners like Jim Brown and Jim Taylor. I weighed 195 pounds at my heaviest in the NFL, and playing corner in those days made a man out of you quickly. You had to be fast enough to cover wide receivers, but strong enough to take on an offensive lineman, and to force running plays back inside.

I couldn't tell you how many concussions I've had, but I had at least three as a rookie, and each one seemed to make me more vulnerable.

"Oh, I remember Irv getting knocked out as a rookie, and it happened way more than three times," Baughan said. "I'd say it was more like eight to ten times. Oh yeah. But as soon as the doctors cleared him, he was right back in there. It might sound bad, but I never worried about it that much. You know why? Because we were all doing it. We all got knocked out sometimes.

I got knocked out one time in Atlanta, but I went back in the game. Different times. That's the way it was."

* * *

My second NFL concussion that I remember occurred while I was throwing a block, and the next one occurred while covering a punt. On that one, I also suffered a fractured jaw. I had to give up eating steaks for a while.

Notice that I still didn't miss the next game. If I were playing today, I know there were times I would not have cleared the concussion protocol. Who knows? Maybe concussions would have forced me to retire sooner than I did.

When I was playing, we only called it a concussion if we got knocked out. I've seen stars, bright lights, and been knocked woozy many times. No wonder I picked up my first nickname with the Eagles. They called me "Paper Head." Guess they thought my head was soft, and that I was easy to knock out. Who knows what kind of permanent damage I was doing to my brain.

My teammates weren't done with the nicknames, either. One day during practice late in the season, it began to snow. My teammate, cornerback Jimmy Carr, looked at the snow and yelled out, "You better go inside Cross, before one of those snowflakes hits you in the head and knocks you out." Everybody started laughing. Then somebody called me "Snowflake," and that nickname stuck with me the rest of the year.

Back then, we didn't even think about the long-term ramifications to our brain. The tougher you were, the better player you were. When you got dinged in the head, you'd get to the bench, get some smelling salts, wait for the cobwebs to clear, and go back into the game.

As a defensive back, we played a lot of single coverage, so it was just you and the man you were defending. I studied film all week and, come Sunday, my mentality was to dominate the receiver in front of me.

I was a physical defensive back, which could have been a problem in today's NFL. Yes, I'm one of those former players who gets infuriated when I watch some of the penalties called on defensive backs today. Sometimes there's just incidental contact, but here comes the flag on the defensive backs. I would've had to adjust quickly.

I also don't like it when I see today's corners who don't like to hit. In my day if a corner didn't tackle, he didn't play. Now if you can cover, it's almost like they cover up for you if you can't tackle. Must be nice.

I started my rookie season as Brookie's backup, and I didn't see much playing time through the first eight games. When I got in, it was mostly on special teams.

But everything changed on November 5, 1961, when we beat the Bears, 16–14, at Franklin Field in Philadelphia. That was the day Brookie's career ended. He suffered a broken leg, a gruesome compound fracture that never healed well enough for him to play again. Brookie's injury meant that I was now in the starting lineup. We were 7–1 at the time, and thought we had a real chance to repeat as NFL champions.

However, losing Brookie was a big blow, and our pass defense wasn't the same. We lost our next two games, trying to make adjustments. But the more game experience I got, the better I played. We beat the Cowboys the following week, 35–13, leaving us 8–3 with three games left in the season.

The next week we played in Pittsburgh against the Steelers. Don't ask me much about that game. I got knocked out cold and suffered the worst concussion I ever had.

It happened on a punt return, which Timmy Brown and I were back to field. Timmy caught the punt and I started to block for him. I took the outside leg of the oncoming Steelers' player, although I have now forgotten who it was. As I threw the block, the player's knee buried into the back of my head.

Goodnight. I was out. I struggled back to the bench but, at that point, I'm told I went into convulsions and almost swallowed my tongue. The next thing I remember is waking up in the hospital. It was the following day. The rest of the team was back in Philly and I was still in Pittsburgh. Ironically, another Steelers player, George Tarasovic, was lying in the hospital bed next to me, getting prepped for knee surgery.

This is the brutal part of football that fans don't see: the morning after. The NFL was already taking its toll on my body—especially my head. I was still a young man, a rookie at my physical peak. But the longer I played, the more my body began to slowly deteriorate. It's like that for all players. As the seasons go by, it takes you longer to recover from injuries, and injuries often occur more frequently. It's a struggle to get out of bed the morning after a game. Sometimes you can't even remember why a certain part of your body hurts—but you know it does, and you want the pain to stop.

I was not released from the hospital in Pittsburgh until Tuesday, two days after the game. For some of those two days I was in and out of consciousness. My first wife, Yvonne, had already traveled from Philadelphia to the hospital in Pittsburgh to see me. I guess this was her "Welcome to the NFL" moment. We had only been married a few months. She had been waiting for me at the airport in Philly after the game, and when my teammates got off the plane, they had to tell her why I wasn't with them. I felt bad for her, but it wasn't like I was in any condition to call.

I knew Yvonne was scared, but she put up a brave front which I appreciated. She already knew football was a dangerous game. Now she was seeing the risks firsthand.

When I finally made it back to Philadelphia, our team doctor spoke to me in no uncertain terms.

"I'm telling you son, if you get hit that hard in the head again, you might be gone," the doctor said. By gone, I knew what he meant. But I was a football player, and we were facing the Giants for the division championship the following week. I hadn't missed a game all season, and I wasn't about to miss *this* game.

I told the doctor not to tell anybody how bad the concussion was, because I was adamant about playing Sunday.

The risk of suffering a more severe head injury was simply not enough to scare me. The division championship was at stake, and I desperately wanted to take the field with my teammates. Maybe I was rationalizing my injuries, but I figured some of my mishaps were just bad luck. On the concussion I suffered in Pittsburgh, I was blocking for Timmy Brown when somebody's knee caught me in exactly the same spot where I suffered my first concussion in training camp. Maybe my head was a little more sensitive in just that one spot. That's the kind of thing I told myself to justify playing.

At least some people were trying to protect me. Rawlings sent me a new helmet, and the trainer put extra padding in it to help me out. I wasn't allowed to have any contact that week in practice. I know helmet design has come a long way since then, and believe me, it's necessary. I've long believed that how a helmet is built is crucial to providing better protection for players. Maybe I should have been a helmet designer.

On Sunday, even after warming up, I still wasn't sure I was going to play. But when I heard my name announced—"Starting at right corner, No. 27, from Northwestern, Irv Cross"—I said, "Screw it. I'm playing." I put my helmet on, ran out, and played the whole game.

Yes, I know that's crazy. But that's the way it was. I just felt as though I couldn't miss that game. By the way, the Giants still beat us, 28–24. The refs made a couple of bad calls, we finished that season 10–4, and missed the playoffs. We missed Brookie's leadership and presence. I didn't think I played that badly as a rookie—made some plays with two interceptions and two forced fumbles.

After that loss to the Giants, a *Sports Illustrated* article had some nice things to say about our team, and Jerry said some complimentary things about me.

"The Eagles went down, and on the way they probably lost the NFL championship," Roy Terrell of *Sports Illustrated* wrote. "But they went down like champions should, losing only 28–24 and scoring more points against the magnificent New York defense than any team has been able to score this year.

"With Brookshier gone and a rookie named Irv Cross at his position, the problem (of stopping Giants receiver Del Shofner) was far more complicated.

"'Cross has come along wonderfully but he's going to need help,' Jerry said. 'What we plan to do is rotate the secondary completely to cover Shofner. The linebacker, Maxie Baughan, will try to hold Shofner up at the line; then Cross will protect against the flat and the down-and-out. If Shofner goes deep, the safety man on that side, [Bobby] Freeman or [Don] Burroughs, will help out. If the Giants begin to hurt us with [Kyle] Rote or [Joe] Walton, we'll have to try something else. But Shofner is the man we're afraid of."

But deep down, I wasn't afraid of Shofner or any other NFL receiver. When the 1961 season ended, I was certain I could play in the NFL. Even the veteran receivers on my team like McDonald felt I could cover any receiver in the league. And if somebody caught a pass on me, I believed in making them pay with a hard tackle.

"He [Brookshier] and Irv Cross were the two best tacklers I ever saw," McDonald told the *Philadelphia Inquirer* when Brookie died in 1993.

Handling the adversity I faced my rookie season made it clear that I belonged in the NFL. I didn't know how many years I would play, especially with nicknames like "Snowflake" and "Paper Head." But this kid from Hammond, Indiana, was a grown man, playing in a grown man's league.

10

1963: A YEAR TO FORGET

HAVE you ever seen somebody die right in front of you? I almost did. And it happened on a football field, in 1963, during my third year with the Eagles.

It was the season opener and we were hosting the Pittsburgh Steelers. We had a running back named Theron Sapp who didn't mess around when he hit the hole. If Theron had to run over somebody to get an extra yard or two, he'd try.

Well, Theron got the ball and headed into the line. Steelers defensive back John Reger was there to greet him, ready to make the tackle. When Theron lowered his head, the top of his helmet caught Reger right in the throat. Reger went down and didn't get up. I was standing on the sidelines watching, and right away I could tell something was seriously wrong.

Reger had swallowed his tongue. He wasn't breathing. He was knocked out cold. His body was limp on the field, and you could tell players on both teams were panicked.

The attendance for that game was listed as 58,205, but Franklin Field was suddenly silent. You could smell fear in the air.

The medics started working on Reger. It was brutal. They had to punch out some of his teeth so they could free his tongue. They were pounding on his chest.

I don't know how long they really worked on him, but it seemed like around 20 minutes. They finally got him to the point where they felt it was safe to move him, and the game continued. Do you think I wanted to keep playing after seeing something like that?

We were all worried about Reger, but the game went on. It ended in a 21–21 tie, but I honestly don't remember much else about what happened in that game.

Fortunately, Reger was okay. The next day there was a picture of him lying in a hospital bed, with his wife and a nurse standing over him. Reger was holding the forceps they had used to help free his tongue.

In Reger's case, tragedy was averted. But three months later, our country wasn't as fortunate.

On November 22, 1963, President John F. Kennedy was assassinated in Dallas, Texas. It was a Friday, and I heard the news after practice that day while I was still in the locker room. One of my teammates, Nate Ramsey, came into the locker room hollering that Kennedy had been shot. Nate was known for playing jokes all the time, so at first I didn't believe him. I didn't want to. But it was no joke. Unbelievably, the president had been assassinated.

With the country shocked and in mourning, NFL commissioner Pete Rozelle made the horrible weekend even more difficult for the players by deciding that the league would play its games as planned, just two days after Kennedy had been killed.

We hosted the Redskins at Franklin Field, and I'm not sure any of us really wanted to be there. Everyone's emotions were on edge. The night before the game, we had a team meeting to discuss our feelings about playing the game, and decided that we would collect money for the family of J. D. Triplett, the Dallas police officer who had been shot and killed by Kennedy's assassin, Lee Harvey Oswald. But before the meeting was over, a fight broke out between two of my teammates, John Mellekas and Ben Scotti, who had different feelings about Rozelle's decision to play.

Scotti beat the crap out of Mellekas. Just an ugly scene between two teammates struggling to deal with grief.

That's the kind of stuff we were dealing with as we took the field that Sunday, and playing a football game two days after the president was assassinated had to be even tougher for the Redskins. They were coming from Washington DC, where the president's body was lying in state. They were even closer to the situation than we were.

Some guys were actually crying on the sideline before the game started, especially when it was time for the national anthem. There was no music, no singer. The entire stadium sang the anthem a cappella.

Surprisingly to me, the announced attendance was 60,671 for that November 24, 1963, home game. We lost, 13–10. Don't ask me many of the details of that game either, because I don't remember. What I do remember is that while the stadium was filled with people and the temperature was in the mid-40s, I felt cold and empty inside. We were playing because we were told to, not because we wanted to. That's not the true spirit of competition. How could we take other people's minds off what had happened when we couldn't even take our own minds off what had happened?

There was frustration for me off the field as well. My first wife and I found a realtor who took us out to Newtown Square, a suburb of Philadelphia, to look at a house. A white friend of ours was actually going to purchase the property and sign it over to us, kind of as a straw party. However, the person who owned the land lived right next door. When he saw it was us who wanted to buy it, he said, "Irv you're a nice guy, I cheer for you every week, but you can't live next door." That was disappointing, it bothered me, and it turned me off on the whole thing. So we ended up buying a house in New Jersey.

Unfortunately, moving across the bridge from Philly didn't get me away from neighborhood profiling. Where we lived, there weren't a whole lot of lights, and it was a quiet suburban development. So one night I was going home, driving within the speed limit, and I saw headlights behind me. I made a right turn and the headlights kept following me. I made a left, a right, a left, and pulled into my driveway. Suddenly the flashing blue-and-red lights from a police car came on.

I got out of the car and said, "What's this?"

The cop said, "What are you doing?"

I said, "I'm going home, what are you doing?"

It really bugged me that he followed me. It was like I was at some place I shouldn't have been. I'm sure he checked my license plate. I can't even remember what kind of car I had, but it sure wasn't the beat-down car I had in college. Even so, that shouldn't matter. The car was mine, this was my house, and I didn't deserve to be hassled. That night bothered me for the longest time. I was just driving home. Can you imagine if I had really gotten belligerent? If he had put his hands on me? I understand why people react angrily when they are stopped for no reason. Too often, black people are stopped for no reason but the color of their skin.

After he ran my plates and was convinced I really lived there, the guy acted like he was a little embarrassed by it. He said, "I was just checking it out."

"Checking what out?" I asked. "I was just driving home."

We have to work harder to understand each other as people. Nobody should become a statistic just because they are black, because of the kind of typecasting that people do.

It was all part of a terrible year, one that began with so much promise. This was my third year in the NFL, I was firmly entrenched as a starter, and I thought we were going to be pretty good. Boy was I wrong. We were terrible. We finished 2–10–2, and were 0–8–1 over our last nine games.

Regardless of what lineup or strategic changes we tried that year, nothing worked. By the time we played our last game in 1963, I couldn't wait for the season to end. And being forced to play two days after Kennedy's assassination is one of the lowlights I'll never forget.

Years later, Rozelle said the decision to play games that day was a mistake, and it sure felt that way at the time. I had no idea I would get to know Rozelle fairly well in my role on the *NFL Today*. And I certainly had no idea that in 2009, I would be honored with the Pro Football Hall of Fame Pete Rozelle Award, which is given for exceptional contributions to radio and television in professional football.

My life has been full of ironies and unexpected twists like that. Which only strengthens my belief that God always had bigger plans for me than I could've envisioned myself. The 1963 season was tough, but I was determined not to let it keep me down. After all, I never lose my faith.

11

INTRO TO BROADCASTING

PEOPLE often ask me, "How did you get started in broadcasting?"

Here's the answer. My rookie year in the NFL was with the Philadelphia Eagles in 1961.

They had won the NFL championship in 1960, and everybody in Philadelphia was hot to have the Eagles do various things for them. Players would get called to do speaking engagements, and sometimes they'd give a player $25 to $50. Could you imagine Tom Brady doing a speech now because he could make an extra 50 bucks? But back then in the sixties, nobody was making Brady's salary, and $50 went a lot further.

The team's public relations staff was swamped with requests from various organizations, asking for players to make appearances. All the star players had more requests than they could handle.

I was just a rookie cornerback from Northwestern. But I was an Eagle. And in Philly, that made me attractive to people looking for speakers.

It was harder for the local Kiwanis Club to book a star player like Tom Brookshier or Pete Retzlaff for a speaking engagement. But if they wanted Irv Cross, I was available. I told the Eagles public relations staff, "If you get any requests from a legitimate non-profit organization, I'll do it for free." I looked upon that gesture as a way of giving back. I wanted to show my appreciation for reaching the NFL, not even thinking that it would lead to something bigger.

One day I gave a talk to the Kiwanis or Rotary Club, I can't remember exactly which one. But after my presentation had ended, a guy from the audience named Bill Emerson walked up to me, gave me his business card and said, "You have a great voice. You should think about going into broadcasting."

Turns out that Bill worked for WIBG, a Philly radio station. It was a rock-and-roll station at a time when that music was very popular. They had a ton of listeners.

The station was tweaking its format and wanted some news and sports breaks during drive time. They invited me to do the sports breaks, and they were well received by the audience. I don't think it would've mattered who was doing the sports breaks, as the station was so popular that nobody was going to turn the dial. They wanted to hear more music after my segment ended, and being on WIBG definitely gave me some early exposure.

Pretty soon I got a call from a Philly TV station, KYW. They asked me to be their sports director, and I did sports on both radio and TV. When I did TV at KYW, it was the last segment of the eleven o'clock news. The next thing after my segment was *The Tonight Show Starring Johnny Carson*, probably the most popular late-night show of all time.

Our ratings were off the charts, thanks largely to Johnny. A lot of people would tune into our eleven o'clock news, because they wanted to make sure they didn't miss Johnny's monologue when he came on at 11:30. That gave our ratings a boost, which was fine by me.

That early radio and TV experience, while I was still playing in the NFL, set the stage for CBS to call me after I retired. The station manager who was at CBS in Philly had gone to New York, so that was a connection. I joined CBS as an analyst, did that for a few years, and that led to me getting a break with the *NFL Today*.

Back in those days, you had to have some local TV experience before you got a shot on the national level. Very few former players were hired by national networks straight out of retirement.

There were also far fewer network opportunities back in those days. No FOX. No ESPN. No NFL Network. It was a totally different landscape.

Sports television was less confrontational back then. Today it seems more about entertainment than reporting. Everyone expresses their opinion, whether they back it up with facts or not. Everyone wants to argue and scream at each other.

I see plenty of talented people in the business, but the approach of today's shows is totally different. I'd really have to adjust if I was on TV now. I'm not on Twitter. I'm not on Facebook. I also think fantasy football has really changed the approach of how the NFL is covered. Fans are more interested than ever in how individual players perform and what kind of stats they put up. You've got Cowboys fans rooting for Eli Manning to have a big day, because they have Eli in fantasy. That kind of thing didn't happen when I was broadcasting.

CBS News with Walter Cronkite was the main image of the network in the seventies, and it set the tone for journalistic standards. You reported stories. You didn't become part of the story.

I think all of that made me a better broadcaster in the long run. I always had confidence on the air, because I believed I was prepared and knew what I was talking about. I never ran with gossip, and I believed in fact-checking before I just spouted something on air.

When opportunities in broadcasting started to come my way, I was determined to bring pride and preparation to the job. That's what I did when I played. I kept notecards on players when I was a broadcaster, just like I did when I played. When the cameras started rolling, I was ready to roll, just like I was ready on Sunday for the opening kickoff. It was a chance to stay close to the game.

As I began my radio and television work in Philadelphia, I never imagined that it would lead to a national TV job. But one opportunity simply evolved into another. I was pretty raw when I first began on some of those radio reports. When I made mistakes, I always tried to learn from them.

* * *

Coming to Philadelphia worked out better than I ever imagined. People there loved the Eagles, and I loved the city. It was so interesting meeting people from various walks of life, and it was definitely the place where my broadcasting roots were planted.

I worked for the Campbell's Soup company during the offseasons in Philly in the personnel department, and I could have stayed with them if I wanted. Every offseason I was looking for a job opportunity where I could move up the ladder. That work ethic was something instilled in me due to the way I grew up. Campbell's was perfect. Each year they put me in a spot where I continued to grow and advance in the company.

I just wish the Eagles could have won more during my career. I'm proud of the NFL career that I put together as a starting cornerback—nine seasons, 22 career interceptions, and making the Pro Bowl in 1964 and '65. I never missed a game my entire career. Teammates and coaches knew they could depend on me. If I could walk, I would play.

However, my biggest career regret is never winning a championship. I've seen players celebrate titles in locker rooms as a broadcaster. But the ultimate feeling of winning a title as a player? That's an experience I've never had. I think about it every time I see a Super Bowl.

During my nine NFL seasons, I only played on four winning teams. I played in just one playoff game.

My rookie season in Philadelphia is really the closest I ever came to winning a championship. We finished 10–4, second in the Eastern Conference behind the Giants, who were 10–3–1. There were only 14 teams in the NFL back then—seven in the Eastern Conference and seven in the Western. The winners of each conference met for the NFL championship, and the Packers blew out the Giants, 37–0, to win the 1961 title. That began the Packers' run of winning five of the next seven titles under their legendary coach, Vince Lombardi.

After falling just short of playing for the championship in 1961, we played in something they called the "Playoff Bowl" in Miami, between the conference second-place finishers. The Lions beat us in that game, 38–10, but talk about a game being anti-climactic! The NFL got rid of that "Playoff Bowl" after 1969. I know in '61, we referred to it as the "Toilet Bowl."

Except for my rookie season with the Eagles, we were bad. Sometimes we were awful. Following that 10–4 rookie season, we were a combined 16–37–3 over the next four years.

I never got to play for Buck Shaw, who retired as the Eagles' head coach after they won the NFL Championship in 1960. Maybe Shaw had a crystal ball and knew it was time to get out.

Nick Skorich, who replaced Shaw, only lasted three seasons as the Eagles' head coach, and we could never duplicate the success the team had after going 10–4 my rookie year. Let's face it, Lombardi built a dynasty with the Green Bay Packers, and everyone else was playing for second place. The Packers were the measuring stick by which all NFL teams were measured, just like the Patriots are that measuring stick now under Bill Belichick.

Joe Kuharich replaced Skorich as head coach in 1964, and the morale of the team went downhill. Kuharich made some questionable personnel decisions that cost us, and he seemed bent on getting rid of the team's strongest personalities.

Kuharich sealed his doom when he traded quarterback Sonny Jurgensen to the Redskins in exchange for quarterback Norm Snead. No knock against Norm, but Jurgensen is in the Hall of Fame for a reason. In my opinion, he's one of the all-time great pure passers the NFL has ever seen. We all knew Sonny liked to hang out at night, and I don't think Kuharich liked that. Sonny wasn't afraid to speak his mind, even holding out of training camp before the start of the 1963 season. I don't think Kuharich liked that either.

The Eagles were a championship-caliber team when I came to town in 1961, but from 1962 through 1965 we had four straight losing seasons. One of the few highlights of that era came during a game against the Steelers in 1965, when we intercepted nine passes to tie an NFL record. I only had one pick that game, but I was happy to share a record with our defense, on one of the few afternoons when things went our way.

In 1965, I was also on the wrong end of a play that became famous—the first NFL spike after a touchdown. The player who did it was Homer Jones, a blazing fast wide receiver for the Giants who beat me on an 84-yard touchdown pass from Earl Morrell.

Jones said he wasn't trying to embarrass me. But he had seen teammates like Frank Gifford and Alex Webster celebrate touchdowns by throwing the football into the stands, and commissioner Pete Rozelle had fined them $50 for doing so.

So when Homer scored the touchdown on me, instead of throwing the ball into the stands, he spiked it into the turf. Just think, if Homer doesn't beat me for that touchdown, there is no spike, and Homer doesn't go down in history. He should thank me!

"I was fixing to throw it into the grandstand," Jones later told ESPN.com. "But just as I was raising my arm, the reality snapped into my head. Mr. Rozelle would have fined me. So I just threw the ball down into the end zone, into the grass. Folks got excited, and I did it for the rest of my career."

The consistent losing during those years was tough on my pride, as well as on my teammates. Kuharich traded some of the best players we had, and eventually got around to trading me as well. I was dealt to the Rams on June 8, 1966, in exchange for halfback Willie Brown and defensive back Aaron Martin. Maxie Baughan had already been traded to the Rams a month earlier, and it was clear to me that, with Kuharich as the Eagles coach, the future did not look bright.

Neither Maxie nor I agreed with some of Kuharich's game strategy. Both of us thought he blitzed too much, putting us out of position to make plays. Instead of relying on the instincts and experience that Maxie and I had, along with other players on the defense, Kuharich wanted to do things his way.

Maxie got fed up with Kuharich first, which led to him requesting a trade. Los Angeles was a long way from Philly, but he was still glad to be away from Kuharich. When Maxie arrived in Los Angeles, one of the first things he did was tell Rams coach George Allen about me.

"George asked me, 'Is there anybody on your team with the Eagles that can play with us?' Baughan said. I said, 'Coach, there's one man that I'll go to bat for. That's Irv Cross.' He said, 'Well, whatever it takes to get him, we're going to get him.' Irv and I played just about the rest of our careers with each other. George put a lot of faith in me asking for my opinion, but as soon as Irv got out there, George saw Irv's work ethic and how good a player he was, and never regretted it."

After trading me and Maxie, Kuharich tried to defend himself with the press.

"The Eagles don't need stars," Kuharich told *Sports Illustrated*. "We need players whose level of performance does not rise and fall like the stock market. Baughan and Cross are good players, but for one reason or another they were not consistent, and this hurt us."

Seeing comments like that from my former head coach didn't make me feel very good. However, I decided to put Kuharich in the past and to take advantage of my fresh start by playing quality football with the Rams.

During my three years with the Rams (1966–68) under Allen, we won a lot more, and it was a pleasure playing for a coach who knew talent when he saw it. Allen was confident about building a winner in Los Angeles in his first year as a head coach. Every player on the 1966 Rams received a gold pen from Allen, with the word "NOW" engraved on it. One of Allen's gifts was his ability to relate to veteran players. Thanks to the Packers dynasty, there were a lot of great players walking around during the sixties without championship rings. Allen tapped into our desperation to win a title and used it to our advantage.

"I want to win now," Allen told *Sports Illustrated*. "I'm not building for the future. I want some men with polish and know-how. You have to have them to win."

Playing for George was tremendous, but I was never as happy living in Los Angeles as I was in Philadelphia. My then-wife and two daughters didn't move with me to LA. We decided not to uproot them, and that made it difficult for me in Los Angeles off the field.

"I noticed that Irv was more of a loner with the Rams," Baughan said. "Being without his family made it real tough on him. He would come out to the house and eat with us sometimes and you could tell it bothered him. But when it came to playing the games, he was still always ready. That was a given."

After the 1968 season, I told George I wanted to be traded back to Philly, and he worked out a deal so I could finish up my career there. I liked playing for George, but my heart was no longer into playing on the West Coast. I only wished I could have taken George with me.

"I loved playing for the Rams," I told Fran Zimniuch for the book *Philadelphia Eagles: Where Have You Gone?* "Coach Allen was 100 percent a defensive coach. It was wonderful. You go into the huddle and you see "The Fearsome Foursome" on your side—Lamar Lundy, Rosey Grier, Merlin Olsen, and Deacon Jones. It was like I died and went to heaven. We had an awesome defense, but my heart was still in Philadelphia."

Olsen later became an actor, and had great success as a star on the television show *Little House on the Prairie*. Olsen was a great guy off the field, but on the field he was an intimidating combination of size and agility.

I was impressed with Merlin's size and athletic ability like everyone else. But he was also one of the smartest teammates I ever had. There wasn't anything required on a football field that Merlin couldn't do well. He was blessed with so many gifts.

I missed Deacon, Merlin, and the rest of the Rams when I was traded back to Philly, but it was where I felt most comfortable—plus, I was once again with my family. In 1969, I spent one season as a player/coach with the Eagles, playing cornerback and coaching the defensive backs. That was difficult. You did everything a coach does, but you still had to be in shape to play the games. I broke down film, helped with the game plan, but also had to go out there and perform on Sunday. It was mentally draining and made it clear to me that my career was coming to an end.

That was my last season as a player. While we suffered through another losing season, we found a young player who would become a standout for us in wide receiver Harold Jackson. I was a teammate of Harold's with the Rams during his rookie season in 1968, but coach Allen didn't play Harold, which was the norm for rookies in those days unless you were special. When I was traded back to Philly, I told the coaching staff about Harold, and the Eagles traded for him in 1969. Harold responded with 65 catches for 1,116 yards, good enough to make the Pro Bowl. I was glad to see Harold's career get jump-started, and he enjoyed a long NFL career.

In 1970, I was strictly the defensive backs coach with the Eagles, and being a full-time coach took away the sting of no longer playing. During that season, I made another personnel recommendation that didn't work out, when I pressed management to draft John Carlos, the Olympic sprinter, as a wide receiver. The Eagles drafted Carlos in the 15th round of the 1970 draft, hoping his blazing speed would make him the kind of deep threat that Bob Hayes became for the Cowboys.

Carlos is most famous for his black-gloved protest with Tommie Smith on the victory stand at the 1968 Olympics in Mexico City. But I believed he could have a terrific post-track career as a football player. I pushed for the powers-that-be with the Eagles to draft Carlos, although he had never played organized football. Carlos was about 6-foot-3, but he could fly. I imagined him being a serious problem for defenses in situations where he was single covered. I ran track and knew the difference between track speed and football speed. When you ran next to a sprinter in full flight, it was beyond fast. It's like rocket speed.

Carlos had that kind of speed and really wanted to play for us. He was pumped up. Had Carlos stayed healthy, maybe he could have helped us. But during a drill before training camp, he hurt his knee and he was never the same. The experiment with him seemed doomed from the start.

Carlos discussed this in his book *The John Carlos Story: The Sports Moment that Changed the World*, written with Dave Zirin.

"I lasted in the NFL roughly a year and a half. This was just long enough to shred my leg and give me the limp I carry with me to this day. I didn't play long enough to apply for any kind of benefits so the therapy and upkeep for this broken wheel is on me.

"I can still see the moment vividly, like it happened yesterday. Irv Cross and I were running some curl patterns. At the time the stadium surfaces were changing from grass to Astroturf and Philly was no exception.

"Prior to taking the field, we did our drills on grass so if I ran a pattern, every time I planted my foot, it would slide on the grass. But practicing on turf was an entirely different animal that I wasn't prepared to tame. Irv threw a curl pattern to me, throwing it a little to the left. I stretched to catch it and my foot didn't slide on that Astroturf, it just locked. Just as I caught the ball, I heard a sound call up to me from my knee, and it said in a voice as clear as Dinah Washington's, '*pop-pop.*' Just like that. After hearing that '*pop-pop,*' I ran several more patterns, perhaps three or four more drills. Then I said, 'Irv, my leg doesn't feel right.' He said what everyone said back at that time, 'Well, go home and ice it.' It didn't swell up and there was no intense pain at the time. It just had a little puff to it. The next day, it was just immobile. I could barely pull myself out of bed, and everyone told me I needed to get it checked out more thoroughly. It was time to see the team doctor."

So much for having Carlos. Meanwhile, I spent the 1970 season on the Eagles coaching staff and, honestly, I don't remember having much withdrawal from no longer being a player. I was still heavily involved with the game as a coach, working long hours yet truly enjoying what I was doing. I really thought coaching was going to be my future.

All the losing seasons in Philadelphia probably made my nine-year playing career seem longer than it was. But I loved Philadelphia. Still do. I loved the people and the connections I was making, both on and off the field.

I also loved the fans. When you played in Philly, you knew how much the fans cared. Go ahead, boo me with everything you've got if we're not playing well. The way we played when we were losing, we deserved to be booed.

It wasn't the booing that got to me in Philly. It was the losing. There was a lot of tension on our team during the mid-sixties, because we weren't winning and guys were on edge. By booing us, the fans let us know they didn't like the way we were playing. Had we been winning, they wouldn't have been booing.

Whenever the Eagles gave the fans any reason for hope, the city supported the heck out of us. As people in the city embraced me, my broadcasting career moved forward, and I was blessed to have some great mentors, some of the best broadcasters that ever lived. They were kind enough to lend me some of their expertise, and I soaked up their knowledge when I started working for CBS.

12

CHOOSING CBS OVER
THE COWBOYS

I MADE a crucial decision in 1971, when I opted for a career in television over coaching.

It was a tough call between a television offer to join CBS and an offer from the Dallas Cowboys to join Tom Landry's staff as a defensive coach. After coaching the defensive backs with the Eagles as a player-coach in 1969, then as a full-time coach in 1970, I really thought coaching was my future.

After the 1970 season, I got a call from Pete Rozelle, who was the NFL commissioner at the time. The league was making an effort to boost minority hiring, as there were no black head coaches and very few black assistant coaches.

Rozelle had me in mind for an even bigger role. He said, "Irv, there's a club interested in talking to you about a front office position."

That team was the Dallas Cowboys. I had negotiated some contracts for some lower-round draft picks, and had also done

115

some scouting. Originally, I thought I had a chance to move up in the Eagles organization, but our lousy season in 1970, followed by a change in the coaching staff in 1971, had closed that door.

The Cowboys were playing at the Cotton Bowl in 1970, but were planning their 1971 move into Texas Stadium. The Cowboys general manager, Tex Schram, was spending a lot of time with the stadium commission and needed somebody to help him with the day-to-day operations of the club.

Tex wanted to hire me as assistant president of the Cowboys. I told him I'd think about it.

Now this part is dumb, but it's true. I spent most of my career with the Eagles, a team that just hated the Cowboys. I'd like to say my dislike for the Cowboys wasn't part of my thinking, but it was. As much as I respected so many people in their organization, like Tex, Tom, and director of player personnel Gil Brandt a part of me just couldn't see myself working for the Cowboys.

However, Coach Landry made the decision even tougher when he called me personally. He said, "If you don't take the front office job with Tex, why don't you come in and coach the defensive backs?"

I always had tremendous admiration for Coach Landry. He was a film nut just like me. He had looked at some of the defenses we had played in Philly and liked our concepts.

I still wasn't sure about taking the job, so Coach Landry flew to Philadelphia to see me. We met at a hotel in downtown Philly. Which hotel I can't remember, but we talked football all night long. I thoroughly enjoyed it. Landry was a devout Christian and knew that I was too. That resonated with me. I thought that was another sign I should take the job.

Now I had two options with the Cowboys to think about. But then CBS called about joining their network.

Here's what really pushed me toward CBS. For one, I lived in Philadelphia, so going back and forth to New York wouldn't be bad and I wouldn't have to move.

Secondly, when I played for the Rams, Coach Allen told me something I never forgot. He liked me as a player and as a person, and he knew that I was thinking about coaching after my playing career was over.

"Irv, coaches get hired to be fired," he said. "If you go into coaching, you have to figure you'll be moving around a lot. It can be tough on your family. I think you'd make a good coach, but think about that hard before you get into it."

Well, I thought about it and opted to take the job at CBS. It was very tough to say "no" to Tom Landry, but it's a decision I've never regretted.

* * *

After CBS officially hired me in 1971, I started out doing about a half-dozen NFL games as a color analyst. By the next year I was given a full season's worth of games, and during my time working as a color analyst I had some of the greatest broadcasters ever sitting next to me.

The three who helped me the most were Jack Buck, Lindsey Nelson, and Vin Scully.

Having Jack Buck as my play-by-play guy was an education in the profession. Jack was an old-fashioned reporter. He dug for information, he got to know players. He didn't talk off the top of his head. When he said something, he knew what he was talking about.

I swear, if you mentioned one thing about baseball to Jack Buck, he could talk about that subject for hours. He was an encyclopedia.

Jack taught me how to do a broadcast chart, breaking down the rosters so you could see right away with a glance which guys were making various plays. Once you do that, you find yourself going more in-depth with your comments, and you're talking with a lot more knowledge. All of a sudden, *boom*, it's coming out of your head naturally. He was great at helping me organize myself for broadcasts.

Then I had Vin Scully. Yes, Vin Scully was doing some football back then, although most people know him as the play-by-play legend of the Los Angeles Dodgers. Just hearing Scully's voice could put you in a trance. I mean, sometimes I'd be sitting next to him and I was just listening. There was a game going on in front of me, but I just wanted to hear what he was saying. There's something magical about that man's voice, and he spoke in poetic phrases all the time. That was his style.

Then I had Lindsey Nelson, with the crazy sports coats. What a pro he was.

Lindsey and I did the Sun Bowl one year in El Paso, Texas. I had my charts and stuff, but we had an open booth. The wind came and blew everything away—all my charts, all my notes, everything.

I was petrified. I turned around, looked at the stage manager, and said, "What do I do now?"

The microphones were still hot. Fortunately, we were in a commercial.

Lindsey tapped me on the shoulder and gave me a great piece of advice.

"Never say anything in front of a microphone unless you want the whole world to hear it."

I never forgot that. Lindsey never said a word at a game during a commercial break. I used to laugh at him, but why take chances? I've seen so many guys get caught like that. It's easy to have somebody pick up something on a microphone that could be going anywhere. I appreciated all those guys, because all of them really loved what they did, and they were all willing to give me advice.

One of my pet peeves about many of today's broadcasters is that they talk too much. If I could it over again, my dream job would be working as a play-by-play broadcaster, and I'd do it the understated way like the old-schoolers. I admired people like Ray Scott, who used to be the voice of the Green Bay Packers. Or Pat Summerall, who had such a nice rhythm to his telecasts. You only heard from him when you needed to.

In my early days at CBS, I figured the more I worked, the more I would learn. Each year, CBS kept giving me more and more assignments, like the Pan Am Games, NCAA gymnastics, track and field. I also did sports anthologies where you'd go up to Canada and cover stuff like the world lumberjack championships on a show they called the *CBS Sports Spectacular*.

I was also doing some NFL preseason games with the Redskins as an analyst. One of my favorite working partners on those broadcasts was Charlie Stopak, who was a producer at the time for WMAL-TV in Washington DC.

"The thing that struck me about Irv was how prepared he was for every game," said Stopak. "Remember, these were preseason games. I'm telling you, I've seen veteran play-by-play guys show up 10 minutes before the start of a preseason game. But Irv would always be one of the first people at the stadium.

"We did a preseason game up in Buffalo, when Rich Stadium was first opening (1973). Irv came in early, and I saw him walk to every section of the stadium to look, then look down at the field. He wanted to see what the sightlines were like, so when he went on the air he could talk about the look of the new stadium from a fan's perspective, having actually seen it. Commissioner [Pete] Rozelle was at that game, and the play-by-play guy was schmoozing with the commissioner to get noticed, while Irv was out there doing his pre-game homework.

"I thought Irv was a terrific game analyst. He explained things in simple terms, not like today, when they go into all this technical stuff that often doesn't mean anything.

"We did a game in Cleveland once, and the play-by-play guy, Jim Thacker, couldn't make it. We got Irv for the play-by-play, and [former NFL quarterback] Frank Ryan to do the color. I wish I had a tape of that broadcast. It was probably the best pair I ever heard doing play-by-play and color. Both of them were so smart.

"During that same game, they had some kind of halftime show where they turned the lights off. Those stadium lights took a long time to warm up, so it took a while for the third quarter to start. So we put a couple of spotlights on Irv and Frank in the broadcast, and we had them talk about football as the lights came up. It was a 15-minute lesson on football. I kept thinking, *I'm actually learning something from these guys.* It reminded me of when I went to Ohio St., and Woody Hayes would give a talk every week at the student union. Irv cared about the game, and he was smart about it. And that integrity about the game stood out in his broadcasts."

I worked those *CBS Sports Spectacular* assignments with enthusiasm, as I enjoy almost any kind of athletic competition. It also gave me a chance to show my versatility, so that I wasn't perceived as just a "football guy."

The person who brought me to the *NFL Today* was Bob Wussler, president of CBS Sports. Bob was in charge of special events, and he was a guy who thought outside the box, who wasn't afraid to take chances. Bob died in 2010 at the age of seventy-three, but the *NFL Today* will always be a huge part of his legacy, and I owe him for giving me a chance on national television when others would not have.

There are many ex-players on television today, and you can tell that some work hard at it while others don't. But if you really want to be good at television as an ex-athlete, you have some obvious advantages having played the game. First of all, you have actually lived the experience of playing in an NFL game on Sunday afternoon. The announcer who has never been in uniform can't know what that really feels like. The fans who are sitting in front of the television, eating pretzels and chips, think they know what it feels like to be in an NFL game, but they obviously don't. I found that being a former player was helpful, because I could give viewers insight at times into what a player

121

was really thinking, or what a coach was really thinking, because I had been there.

I wanted to talk about football. Players like to talk about football. If there was something the Cowboys or any other team was doing that was tearing people apart, I could break that play down, talk to players and coaches about it, then when fans saw it during a game they'd have a greater appreciation of what was going on. I thought part of my role was to be a teacher. I wanted people to understand more about the games, and the players, they were watching.

I think it's important to take your ego out when you're relaying things to the viewer. I hear guys say things like, "If I was playing in this game, this is what I would do." That's great, but what are the guys on the field doing? And why are they doing it?

Secondly, being a former player gives you credibility with the viewers. As you continue with your job, you must sustain that credibility by being good at your job. But at the start, being a former player gives you an advantage.

"Irv isn't just intelligent, he's smart," said Maxie Baughan. "Some people don't know how to use their intelligence. Irv does. He would never go on a show like the *NFL Today* without being totally prepared. I knew that, and that's why I knew he'd be good. He was always ready as a player. Why would announcing be any different?"

I spent a lot of time at NFL Films when I was on the *NFL Today*, always breaking down tape and learning new things. Football is always evolving. You may have known the game well as a player, but trends change, coaches change, players change. So I called and interviewed people in person every week for our segments on Sunday. That gave me confidence on the air, because I collected much of the information for the segments myself.

"Irv was the pioneer," former ESPN analyst Tom Jackson told Broncos.com, after winning the Pete Rozelle Award for Broadcasting in 2015. "Irv Cross did it, did it well, had great impact on the viewing audience and paved the way for somebody like me to get a shot and get on TV."

Here's another advantage a former player has in television that is often overlooked. You're used to being part of a team. There's a lot of truth to the cliché "football is the ultimate team sport." You can't succeed on that field, no matter how good you are, without your teammates. There are people in television, and from all walks of life, who come to a job almost always thinking about themselves. And they can be highly successful as a lone wolf who doesn't really interact that much with people they work with.

However, I took the approach in television that I was still part of a team; that I was willing to work with others to help the final product be as good as it could be. And I think the reputation I built for taking that approach helped me land the *NFL Today* job.

One person I enjoyed working with was Ed Goren, a coordinating producer at CBS Sports during the seventies before moving on to oversee FOX Sports television.

"Anybody you talked to about that show will tell you that Irv provided a much-needed dose of sanity," said Ed Goren. "No matter how much they might be going back-and-forth behind the scenes, when they were on the air it was magical.

That show created four national personalities, which just doesn't happen.

"Wussler's idea to put that combination together took the *NFL Today* to another level. The shows today are really not that much different. Go out on the street and ask somebody which weekday morning show they watch—the *Today Show*, *Good Morning America*, whatever. Then ask them why they like it. It won't be because of the graphics, the music, the set, or the features. They like the people on camera. That's where the money is.

"People liked Brent, Irv, Phyllis, and the Greek. They liked them together then, and people would like them together now. When you look back at old clips of some shows, you think, 'That show wasn't as good as I remember.' But when you look at old clips of Brent, Phyllis, Irv, and eventually the Greek, you think, 'That show was darn good.'"

Wussler had been in Chicago for a while and was familiar with Brent's work as a sports anchor in Chicago. Phyllis was known to Wussler because he had done the Miss America contest when she won it.

When Wussler saw me on the air, he thought I could handle the job. But I have to admit, when I first heard the concept of the *NFL Today* show, I thought I might be happier remaining in the broadcast booth.

"I thought the action was at the game sights," I told the *Washington Post* after my run on the *NFL Today* had ended. "[But] before you knew it, the show took on its own energy and direction, and it really took off."

Years later, I was told that my reputation for being easy to work with was another reason I was targeted for the *NFL Today* show.

"I remember one Thanksgiving on the *NFL Today*, when my mother was visiting," said Rich Podolsky, a former writer on the *NFL Today*. "The studio was quiet, and it was one of those rare times when you could have a relative on the set hanging out. So I brought my mother to the set so she could watch us do the show.

"Riding home, I asked her what she thought. The first thing she said was, 'Boy that Irv Cross, what a wonderful guy, the nicest man.' It struck me that of all the personalities she met that day—Brent, Phyllis, the Greek—the one who was probably considered the least flamboyant on the set was the one who made the biggest impression on my mother.

"I'm also from Philadelphia and I remember Irv as a player for the Eagles. I was a kid in high school selling programs at Eagles games. I'd walk along the sidelines and I'd see Irv warming up before the game. He was a tremendous athlete. He'd always smile at the kids who yelled for his attention. I've got nothing but great memories of Irv. He's so nice all the time, because that's who he truly is."

Wussler's vision for the *NFL Today* was a fast-paced, entertaining show with distinct personalities. It would have some news, but would also have personality profiles, which either myself or Phyllis would handle. Brent would be the point man—the person who would lead the way. Jack Whitaker was the fourth person on the *NFL Today* when it began, and Jimmy "The Greek" Snyder didn't join us until 1976.

Jack was a brilliant reporter. He was another guy I just loved listening to. He'd have a two-minute segment where he'd make a philosophical statement about the game or an individual. You'd be mesmerized by every word he spoke. Jack was a real pro.

"Wussler was a very creative guy, and I think he thought the time was right to do a show like that, and to do it live," Brent Musberger said. "He was hopeful that the three personalities, myself, Irv, and Phyllis, would mesh. They did, and that allowed him to bring in the Greek, and to mix in the gambling element.

"Our four personalities were entirely different. The mixture together, the combination of all four of us, was what made it so unique. But without a shadow of a doubt, it was Wussler's creation. And then selecting Mike Pearl as producer was another great move, because he felt that Pearl could get along with the different personalities. He could handle the bombast of the Greek. He could handle working with a former Miss America. He could handle me and Irv. Wussler had a lot of foresight putting this combination together."

As they were putting things together for the *NFL Today*, I came up to New York to talk to Wussler about the show. So we're talking, and the meeting is going well. But remember this was the seventies. The movie *Shaft* had already come out, and I started to get the feeling they had targeted me for a Shaft-like personality. You know, cool, hip, whatever. The big hats, the leisure suits.

When the meeting was over, they took me to this men's store in Manhattan around 42nd Street and 7th Avenue to pick out a wardrobe. There was a woman with us who picked out a light-blue leisure suit with dark stiches around the collar. Then she gets a blue and white silk shirt. Then she gets a gold medallion for me to wear down the middle of my chest. I don't have a lot of chest hair, but you were going to see what little I had if I opened up that silk shirt and I wore that medallion.

This was my thought process as I walked into the changing room to put these clothes on that I would never buy for myself. The potential for the *NFL Today* sounded good. I loved the chance it would give me to interview players and to talk football on a national stage. But this wardrobe thing was rubbing me the wrong way. There's no way I was wearing these clothes on national TV.

I was thinking about those clothes on the train ride back to Philadelphia. So when they offered me the job, I told them I had to think about it. I had a rule of thumb anyway, that I wouldn't respond to any job offer unless I thought about it for at least 24 hours.

When I called Wussler back I said, 'Bob, I can't go on television dressed like that. I wear a sport coat and tie. I never dress like that. I don't know what you want me to be, but that's not me. If you want somebody to look like that, you ought to get Sammy Davis Jr. or Bill Cosby. They're entertainers, comedians. I'm not."

Wussler said, "Well, OK Irv, why don't you think about it some more, and I'll get back to you soon."

A couple of days later he called me back.

"C'mon up to New York, you know we want you, and you can dress however you want."

I was happy. But here's what I didn't know. The network had already committed to like 220 stations for the show, with Brent, Irv, and Phyllis as the talent. They were locked in, because CBS had already committed to me as part of the talent for at least a year. They were already stuck with me.

If I had balked at the clothes and said no right away, I'm convinced I would've never been on the show. But because I waited, and because they had already committed to me, it was too late for them to make a change. So I got to be on the show and wear what I wanted.

I wanted to do the show, but not at any cost. If I'm going on this show as a black man, a lot of people are going to be watching. I wanted to make a strong representation for the people who would be watching me, especially black people who'd be looking at me on TV—or those who had prior opinions of what a black man on television looks like.

Somebody at CBS saw me as something I wasn't. I had already been on the air for four years. I had done all these broadcasts, I had a certain style, people saw how I operated and they liked that. But now that I was going to be in the national spotlight, all of a sudden they wanted this different cat. I was really angry about that for a while. I knew if I went on the show and tried to act like some jive dude I really wasn't, I wouldn't last a week. But who did they really want? What were they really looking for? They were looking for what they thought would work, what they thought viewers expected or wanted to see from a black analyst.

So I joined the *NFL Today* knowing I had to be a little more careful because I was black. I never hung out with the other people on the show after it was over. No hanging out at the bar, no going out for dinner.

For one thing, I don't drink. So why should I go out to a bar, whether it was with Phyllis, Brent, or Jimmy?

I guess they thought I may have been aloof or something—until they got to know me better. I never told people on the show that I didn't drink. I just didn't go out.

"I'm well aware that Irv doesn't drink," said Musburger, laughing. "We tried to give him reason to drink, but he never did. He and [former University of Indiana basketball coach] Bob Knight are the two people I've worked with who don't drink. Irv was just a lot nicer about it than Bob was when he told you he didn't want to drink."

They didn't know about my father, about the drinking problem he had. From the time I was ten years old, I swore that I would never smoke or drink. So I never did.

If I was going to be part of the show, I was going to be me. I was fully prepared for being the only black person in the room, having experienced that going to college at Northwestern, and from being one of the few black students in my high school. Being the only black person in a crowd was something I could handle.

However, having a black person in the room was new for some people at CBS.

Here's a story that kind of set the tone for me on the show.

After taping our first show, we go in for our meeting. Duke Struck, our director for the show is there. He worked in Washington for some local shows, and I knew him from doing Redskins games.

We're at this meeting, and Duke says, "Irv, you don't sound like a black guy."

I said, "What do you mean?"

"You know, you don't sound like a black guy."

"Duke, how does a black guy sound?"

The meeting just stopped. There was about 30 seconds of tension in there, no talking.

Everybody else in the room probably wanted to get out.

Then I said, "Hey man, I know what you're talking about. I took speech classes at Northwestern. I graduated with pretty high honors. I know how to communicate with people. A lot of people can't. I can. And you know what Duke? A lot of black folks sound just like me. Everybody in my family sounds just like me."

The comment aggravated me at the time, but I knew Duke, and I knew he didn't mean anything by it. I guess he was trying to figure out how I could be so articulate.

It's just ignorance. Many people I was working with had no close relationships with black people, so they assumed stereotypes to be true.

Years later, thinking about a white guy, telling me that I don't talk like a black guy, makes me laugh. And in a strange way, that meeting broke the ice for me on that show. From then on, everybody knew that what they heard from me was Irv Cross talking like Irv Cross, and that they'd be getting it every week. I had studied. I had prepared. When the *NFL Today* gave a black man an opportunity on national television, I was ready.

13

ME AND MISS AMERICA

MY friendship with Phyllis George, which has lasted more than thirty years, was one of the best things about working on the *NFL Today*.

Phyllis's life has been amazing. She has been a pioneer in television, Miss America (1971), and the First Lady of Kentucky among other things. In addition, she has done a lot of work and fundraising for a variety of worthwhile causes. But more than that, she's a fantastic person.

I don't think Phyllis gets enough credit for being a terrific interviewer. Players just felt comfortable talking to her, and she could get quotes from them that the rest of us couldn't.

One of the best examples was when Phyllis interviewed Cowboys quarterback Roger Staubach, who had this straight-laced image and deservedly so. But, somehow, Phyllis got Roger to talk about his sex life on national television—in 1975!

Phyllis got that response by asking Roger a great question.

"Roger, you have an All-American image. You're kind of a straight guy. Do you enjoy it, or is it a burden?

Here's how Staubach responded.

"You interviewed Joe Namath, and everyone in the world compares me to Joe Namath as far as the idea of off the field, he's single, bachelor-swinging, I'm married with a family and he's having all the fun. I enjoy sex as much as Joe Namath. Only I do it with one girl."

It's one of those quotes you remember, especially coming from Staubach. Phyllis also had a great interview with Jets quarterback Joe Namath, in which Namath admitted his struggling Jets team wasn't very good.

"We are a very inconsistent football team, not a very good football team at this point," Namath told Phyllis. "In fact, we're terrible."

"You don't have much time," Phyllis said to Namath.

"Much time for what?" an irritated Namath shot back.

"You say consistency, how long does it take to get the consistency?" said Phyllis, continuing to press on.

"I don't know," Namath said, curtly, but candidly.

That was good television, and it was clear from Day 1 that Phyllis could hold her own. I saw her cry. I saw her angry. But I never saw her unable to do her job well.

Meanwhile, I had no idea what kind of genuine person Phyllis was when they first put her together with me and Brent. But I quickly learned that Phyllis was close to her family, and a Texan at heart. She was a diehard Cowboys fan. Phyllis just loved those Cowboys, and the fact that a former Eagle like myself, and a Cowboys fan like Phyllis, could get along says something about the respect we had for each other!

The first couple of weeks of the show, we went down to Denton, Texas, where Phyllis was born and raised. During that trip, I got to meet Phyllis's mother, who was also a delightful lady.

When Phyllis was Miss America, she always had people to help her do different things when she made appearances. But I think her mother knew that doing the *NFL Today* was going to be a different challenge. So at some point in the visit, Phyllis's mom pulled me aside and made it clear she was depending on me to look out for her daughter.

"Phyllis is going to be talking to all those football players? I don't know," her mom said.

"I'm expecting you take care of her, and make sure she's going to be OK."

What else could I say but, "OK, Mrs. George." From then on, I was like her big brother at work.

Phyllis bought into that, too. She felt comfortable with me, which became more important after Jimmy the Greek joined the show and had a rocky relationship with Phyllis. However, Phyllis and I always got along great. She trusted me, and our friendship has lasted all these years. We always felt at ease with each other. I'll let her speak about how she felt.

"Irv was always there for me as a friend," said George. "He was just so consistent in the way he treated people. I don't think Irv's ever been in a bad mood.

"What I knew about Irv before I met him was that he had been a terrific football player. What I didn't know was that he was a fabulous person. For all of us, being chosen to be on the *NFL Today* was a huge step in our careers. I majored in communications in college, and I wanted to get into broadcasting, even though I didn't know it would be sports.

"The chemistry with the three of us—Brent, Irv, and myself, caught on quickly. The Greek hadn't arrived yet, and the three of us bonded. Brett was the traffic cop, I did the human interest stuff, and the players seemed to open up to me. And Irv could break down anything that happened on the field because he understood the game so well. We all found our niche. And once we did, everything clicked, between ourselves, and with the audience.

"It was all new, it was different, and it worked. It was a long shot by Bob Wussler to put Brent, Irv, and myself together, but it was genius. Looking back, I think it was the greatest job I ever had. I worked from, what, September through the Super Bowl? Really, I didn't have to work half the year. I had a dream job, if you want to know the truth.

"I honestly didn't realize the impact that the *NFL Today* had until we were a few years into it. We were coming into people's living rooms, and they viewed us as part of their family. Simply put, working with Irv was just a total joy. I can honestly say that I've never met anyone nicer in my life. He just maintained his cool through the storms surrounding all of us. He just loved being on that show. I think when I left after ten years, I broke up the family in a way. When we were on the road during championship games, playoff games, I knew the more time I spent with Irv, the better I'd feel. Because he was always so kind.

"Irv and I also knew that we were both playing important roles. Irv was the first African American in that position. He was good, but being a pioneer had to be extra pressure for Irv.

It's not something he ever talked about with me, but it had to be there.

"I had pressure on me for different reasons. I was the first woman in such a prominent role on a sports show. Bob Wussler told me to have fun, but he also told me I couldn't just go for cute interviews. I had to get people to talk. When I started, I wasn't guaranteed that it was going to be long-term for me. It was like a 13-week trial until I proved I could handle it. So I had to be innovative, like throwing the football with guys, or one time I did an interview jogging with George Allen when he was coach of the Redskins.

"I felt plenty of women were counting on me, and I'm such a competitor, I was determined not to fail. That's probably another reason why Irv and I bonded. With both of us in pioneering roles, we had each other's back."

With Brent, Phyllis, and myself, the *NFL Today* got off to a roaring start in 1975, and the three of us had a great working relationship.

"The chemistry that I saw between them most of the time was great, even after the Greek came, and I don't think that's emphasized enough," said George Veras, a producer at CBS Sports from 1981–94. "Brent had incredible retention of information and energy. He was the maestro. Jimmy was the character, the background guy that people recognized in clubs, who had many, many friends in the league. He was a very generous man and dealt with personal tragedies. He was loveable most of this life, although in the end he was beat down and lost the sparkle he had.

"Nobody could deny that Phyllis was brought on to appeal to women. But she was good. She wasn't meant to be the X's-and-O's person and she was a breakthrough for television.

"Irv was like Tom Jackson, the articulate ex-player who loved the game, knew the game from a technical point of view, and knew the players. On top of that, Irv was incredibly friendly.

"Brent didn't like pre-rehearsed answers. So Brent's way of creating spontaneity was to throw a different question at any of the three of them. At times, that would irritate Jimmy, because he really didn't want to be surprised. Phyllis would sometimes just handle it by laughing. Irv would smile, but he could play along with Brent and answer the question. He brought the same qualities as a team player that made him a good football player."

We weren't a hard-hitting news show, but we were entertaining. And because all of us had contacts around the league, we could get inside information.

"All four of us on the show are close to at least one owner," Brent told the *Washington Post* in 1983. "Jimmy Snyder is close to Al Davis in Oakland, Phyllis is close to Tex Schramm and Tom Landry in Dallas, nobody is closer to the Eagles and the [Leonard] Tose family in Philly than Irv Cross, and I know the [George] Halas people very well from my years in Chicago."

By 1976, CBS was fully committed to making the *NFL Today* the biggest and best pregame show ever. Before Super Bowl X between the Steelers and Cowboys in Miami, we did a

90-minute pregame show on a moving yacht while it was traveling down Biscayne Bay!

CBS even put out a press release to make sure everyone knew we were pulling out all the stops for the Super Bowl X pregame show.

"CBS television network will go down to the sea in a ship for its coverage of Super Bowl X on Sunday, January 18, beginning at 12:30 p.m.," the press release read.

Brent Musberger, Phyllis George, and Irv Cross, hosts of the *Super Bowl Sunday Special*, will step aboard the *Thomas Cat*, a 57-foot Chris Craft Constellation, at the Palm Bay Club in Miami. CBS Sports leased the craft from Neil Cargile Jr., a Nashville, Tennessee, businessman-sportsman.

As the *Thomas Cat*, to be renamed the *Super Bowl Special*, cruises down Biscayne Bay toward the Orange Bowl, the *Super Bowl Sunday* hosts will entertain and interview celebrities from the worlds of sports and show business.

Included in the party-time festivities will be remote pickups and interviews from such locations as the Fontainebleau Hotel, the Miamarina, and the Bowl Bar, a watering hole across from the game site.

The *Super Bowl Sunday* hosts, who will utilize the 50-yard line presidential box for halftime and postgame activities, will arrive at the Miamarina in time to sample a fur and bikini fashion show for players' wives before a helicopter picks them up for a televised ride to the Orange Bowl, about two miles away.

Along with a look at points of interest and late pre-game developments, the broadcast will show highlights of the past nine Super Bowls.

So up to kickoff time between the Pittsburgh Steelers and the Dallas Cowboys, all the ballyhoo and high spirits already associated with the week will be summarized in CBS Television Sports Network's own *Super Bowl Special Sunday*.

We had Joe Namath and some other athletes and stars come aboard to be interviewed. We showed clips from some of the Super Bowl parties during the week, where celebs like Alice Cooper and Raquel Welch were hanging out. We moved smoothly over the water toward the stadium while doing the show. Then when the show ended, Brent, Phyllis, and I boarded a helicopter that took us to the stadium. Not exactly the worst day of my life!

In addition to the three of us, Gary Bender, Don Criqui, Alex Hawkins, Paul Hornung, Sonny Jurgensen, Al Michaels, Johnny Morris, Lindsey Nelson, Hank Stram, and Johnny Unitas were all part of the CBS broadcast team for the game.

Wussler seemed elated with how the glitzy production came off. I had never done interviews on a yacht before, but what the heck?

"One of the major problems with Super Bowl telecasts has been that the game is taken too seriously," Wussler told *Sports Illustrated*. "I feel you need only two main announcers to cover the game itself, and we assigned Pat Summerall and Tom Brookshier. We will have nobody down on the sidelines as others have in the past, because I don't remember anyone ever telling me anything interesting from there."

We were pushing the limits for what viewers would watch leading up to a big game, and it was working. I still had no idea that Super Bowl Sunday would become like a national holiday. But I think our show played a small part in helping momentum move in that direction.

"People would watch anything connected to that game," CBS executive producer Mike Pearl told *Rolling Stone* magazine. "As time has gone by, in addition to the X's and O's factor, there was more entertainment thrown in as well. That was also in concert with the NFL, because they found that they could do some things entertainment-wise, inside and outside the stadium. But it was just a very simple formula that everybody caught on with."

Little did we know, the dynamic on the set of the *NFL Today* was about to change in a very big way. That's when Jimmy "The Greek" Snyder came aboard. Neither Phyllis, nor myself, nor Brent had any idea how much "The Greek" would eventually shake things up.

14

FIGHT NIGHT

THE *NFL Today* was so popular that at one point, even when something went bad, it still turned out good.

A perfect example was the bar fight between Brent and the Greek in 1980, which took place at a Manhattan bar called "Peartrees" on a Sunday night in October. I've heard stories about the fight hundreds of times, as I wasn't at Peartrees when it happened. It's hardly shocking that I wasn't in a bar, since I don't drink. I also didn't hang out with Brent and Jimmy off camera.

Nothing personal. I liked both Brent and Jimmy, but staying in New York after the show wasn't my thing—not with the hectic schedule I had during football season. During a typical week, I was on a plane somewhere by Tuesday to do interviews for the following weekend's show. I might get back home to Philly by Friday, but on Saturday I was headed back to New York to get ready for the show on Sunday. When we wrapped the show on Sunday evening, I was eager to get back to Philly to spend what little time I had at home with my family.

Apparently, Brent and the Greek needed to unwind after that particular show. They just so happened to end up in the same bar, which led to their fight.

The tension on the show that day was thick. In fact, for some time, there had been problems behind the scenes.

It seemed as though the more popular the Greek became, the more airtime he wanted. Phyllis had grown to dislike the Greek, and for good reason. He was intentionally crude to her. That always flustered Phyllis, sometimes to the point where she would break down and cry. But Phyllis was tougher than she seemed, and she appealed to our audience. People wanted to hear from her. She wasn't about to yield some of her airtime to the Greek.

Meanwhile, I always had more material than they were using on the show. Most of my segments were only two or three minutes. I can remember Brent saying on many occasions, "We need to use more of Irv." But there wasn't enough time for all of us to do everything we wanted. Brent had to keep the show moving. Airtime was always an issue, and the Greek, more than anybody, thought he was getting an unfair piece of the pie.

This was the year that Phyllis returned to the show, after her two-year absence. To convince Phyllis to come back, I think she had been assured by CBS that Jimmy wouldn't be as much of a problem for her as he was before. But Phyllis and Jimmy still weren't getting along. Now Brent and Jimmy weren't getting along either. A story in the *Washington Post* described the atmosphere on the set as follows:

"Musberger has the unhappy task of quarterbacking the team of Phyllis George, Jimmy the Greek, and Irv Cross. Irv never complains, he does his job and gets on with it . . .

but Phyllis and Jimmy are always scrapping over how many minutes they get on the air, and because it's up to Brent to bring them into the conversation they tend to blame him.

"Phyllis was putting pressure on Brent all day for more airtime, and that made both Brent and Jimmy sore . . . but Jimmy got even more mad because to him it looked like Brent decided in her favor."

"That's all true," Musberger confirmed. "Jimmy thought I was giving Phyllis too much damn airtime."

The discord between Brent and Jimmy continued at Peartrees, with Jimmy accusing Brent of siding with Phyllis. One thing led to another, and Jimmy took a swing at Brent. From what I'm told, Jimmy didn't connect, but some words were exchanged before they were separated.

Of course, this was New York. This was a bar. And there was no way the fight wouldn't become public knowledge.

The next day the fight made headlines in papers from coast to coast. That's how big we had become. Brent had a funny quote in the *Washington Post*, saying, "Fortunately for my jaw, the Greek's punch is as accurate as his handicapping has been lately . . . wide to the left."

When I heard about the fight, I wondered if it would further damage Brent and Jimmy's working relationship. Nobody wanted a feud between them to linger.

Whatever concerns I had disappeared the next weekend. I think the show's producers took the right approach by deciding to joke about the incident on air to diffuse the tension. The next Sunday, Phyllis rang a bell, as if she was ringing two boxers into the ring. Brent called Jimmy "Jimmy The Knockout," and he wore a boxing glove on one hand as he pointed to Jimmy's predictions.

"They were going to fire the Greek for that incident," Musberger said. "I talked a couple of the executives out of it. I thought we could get beyond it. It was like two brothers fighting. 'Please don't fire him,' I said. It's not what the show needs. It's not what the Greek needs. And I don't think it's what I need.

"I thought about it a lot. I told Bob Wussler, 'What we need to diffuse this is some humor. Get some boxing gloves. Get a bell. We're not coming out boxing. We're coming out smiling.' That was a time where I was pretty adamant about how I wanted things to be handled, and it worked out."

Even Jimmy participated in the clowning on air.

"Neither Don King, nor Bob Arum, will offer $10 million for a rematch between me and the Greek," Brent said. I just sat back and laughed. I thought they handled the whole thing beautifully.

The ratings for that week's show were sky high. It seemed we could do no wrong. People loved our show, and the scuffle between Brent and Jimmy only made people more curious.

I never got caught up in the ratings, but I knew we had a good thing going. It was like the *NFL Today* had a Teflon coating. When we smiled and laughed together, people watched. When we brawled, people watched. That kind of magic is hard to pull off. But the *NFL Today* had it.

15

ME AND THE GREEK

IF you know the *NFL Today*, you know Jimmy "The Greek" Snyder. Or at least you think you know Jimmy.

I've been asked about the rise and fall of Jimmy "The Greek" many times. At his pinnacle, Jimmy was the country's most famous bookmaker and a national TV star, one of my partners on the *NFL Today*. But Jimmy died a lonely and disgraced man—branded a racist thanks to senseless comments he made.

Let's start with the 1988 interview that cost Jimmy his career. He was having lunch at a restaurant in Washington DC, and agreed to be interviewed by a TV reporter (Ed Hotaling of WRC) about civil rights in sports. It was the weekend of Dr. Martin Luther King's birthday, and we were in town for the Vikings-Redskins NFC Championship game.

Here are the remarks that Jimmy made in that interview, remarks he would regret for the rest of his life.

"Well, they've got everything; if they [(blacks] take over coaching like everybody wants them to, there's not going to be anything left for white people.

"I mean all the players are black; I mean the only thing that whites control is the coaching jobs . . . The black talent is beautiful; it's great; it's out there. The only thing left for whites is a couple of coaching jobs.

"There are ten players on a basketball court. If you find two whites, you're lucky. Either four out of five or nine out of ten are black. Now that's because they practice and they play and they practice and play. They're not lazy like the white athlete.

"The black is a better athlete to begin with, because he's been bred to be that way. Because of his high thighs and big thighs that go up into his back. And they can jump higher and run faster because of their bigger thighs, you see.

"I'm telling you that the black is the better athlete and he practices to be the better athlete and he's bred to be the better athlete because this goes all the way back to the Civil War when, during the slave trading, the owner, the slave owner would breed his big woman so that he would have a big black kid, see. That's where it all started."

I can't remember exactly where I was that day; the moment when Jimmy was ruining his career. But when I got to my hotel, I remember my phone starting ringing. A reporter from the Associated Press asked me for a comment. When he told me what Jimmy had said, I was shocked.

"They don't reflect the Jimmy the Greek I know, and I've known him for almost thirteen years," I told the Associated Press.

I feel the same way today. I don't think he was a racist. I'll go to my grave feeling that way. I had seen Jimmy in so many conversations, and a racist viewpoint from him simply didn't come across to me. When a black player was better than a white player, he'd say so with no hesitation.

There's also no denying that Jimmy was a huge part of the show—that some viewers tuned in just to see him. He gave the *NFL Today* its edgy element—a gambler who was telling you which team he liked, and by how much. He would never mention point spreads, but it wasn't hard to read between the lines. When Jimmy said, "I like the Falcons by a field goal," or "I like the Cowboys by a touchdown," you knew what he meant.

To this day, I have no idea how good Jimmy really was at handicapping games. I know he had a close relationship with former Raiders owner Al Davis, and I suspect that whatever inside information Jimmy was getting, he was getting from Al.

There was no denying Jimmy had charisma. He loved the spotlight, and the camera loved him back. When the *NFL Today* was in its heyday, and you went anyplace with Jimmy, he immediately became the center of attention . . . and he loved every minute of it. He had commercial deals and speaking engagements, and he was probably the most popular personality on the show.

I'm not saying Jimmy was easy to work with. He wasn't, especially for Phyllis and Brent. Jimmy could be a bully verbally to Phyllis, and he knew that would upset her.

"I don't think Jimmy enjoyed a woman being on the program," George said when interviewed for *Bearing the Cross*. "That's another reason why I was so glad Irv was on the show. In some ways, he was like my protector. I knew I could turn to him for support, because he knew what I was going through with Jimmy.

"If I told you some of the inappropriate sexual comments that Jimmy made, you would cringe. Jimmy was a complicated person. When he joined the show I believe he had already lost two children to cystic fibrosis, and then he lost a third child after I knew him. I can't imagine what that was like for him. I told him that I was heartbroken for him, and that broke the ice between us near the end of the show.

"But for the most part, we didn't get along. Irv could deal with him better than I could.

"One time, Jimmy brought tears to my eyes with something he said about my husband. We were about to go on the air, and I had gone back off the set to compose myself. Our executive producer, Mike Pearl, came running out to me and said, 'Phyllis, you need to get back out there. We're live. And we're a family.'

"I said, 'Really, a family?'

"Mike said, 'Yes. A dysfunctional family. But a family.'

"Things got so bad with Jimmy that I called my attorney, Ed Hookstratten. Ed called CBS and said, 'Either Phyllis has to go, or Jimmy has to go.'

"We reached a compromise where Jimmy would come in early, tape his segments, then I'd come in later and I wouldn't have to speak with Jimmy. That worked for me. I didn't have to see him."

The dynamic between Jimmy and Brent also had tension. Jimmy didn't really understand many things about television.

I'll give you an example. Near the end of one show, Brent is winding it down, trying to sign off, and he makes a comment about a game that's coming up later. Well, Jimmy is on the other side of the desk, trying to get Brent's attention because he's trying to say something.

It wasn't the right time for that. Brent is locked in, trying to sign off. So he never gives Greek a chance to say whatever he wanted to say.

After the show, Greek says to Brent, "You didn't come to me. I had something to say."

Brent says, "I couldn't. I didn't have time."

Jimmy didn't like it. So he moped the rest of the day, and we were on the air for like eight hours. Not a good day.

I think that's the same day Brett and Jimmy got into the fight at Peartrees. However, Jimmy and I always got along well. I always thought he respected me. I never sensed he was a racist.

In fact, I know for a fact that Jimmy donated money to black colleges for scholarships before all this happened. Maybe he thought he could get information about players in return, but for whatever reasons, I know he made those donations. I think he had a genuine soft spot for minority kids. My belief is that he always had a thing for the underdog. He may have felt like an underdog himself, as a Greek kid growing up poor.

I also know Jimmy had a big heart and had overcome plenty of personal tragedy. He lost three children to cystic fibrosis. Imagine the pain that caused him.

However, there's no way I can defend the comments he made. When I watched the interview, I clearly saw that the more he said, the deeper the hole he dug for himself. The next day when I arrived at the set, Jimmy the Greek was gone—for good.

CBS had standards. *CBS News with Walter Cronkite* was the image of that network for years. Things had to be done professionally. You report stories. You didn't become a part of the story.

"We didn't hire Jimmy to be a genealogist," said Neal Pilson, president of CBS Sports from 1981–83, and 1986–95. "We didn't hire him to opine on DNA. That became a huge controversy that blew up overnight. We felt we had to take Jimmy off the show. We took him off the pregame the following day, and he never worked for us again, and we didn't renew his contract. Most people think we fired Jimmy. We actually didn't. We paid him until the end of his deal and didn't exercise a renewal. We made the decision that we couldn't put Jimmy on the air the next day."

"One of the sad ironies about the whole situation is that a technical difficulty set up Jimmy's demise," said former *NFL Today* executive producer Ted Shaker. "Mikhail Gorbachev (former soviet leader) was in DC visiting. We used to do these comedic pieces with Jimmy and, for this one, we were going to have Jimmy riding down the street in a limousine through a crowd of people like Gorbachev.

"But when the camera crew went to shoot the video of Jimmy riding down the street, the camera broke. Somebody had to run back to the CBS News bureau to get another camera. So somebody suggested to Jimmy that he should go have lunch, and we would shoot the piece afterward. That's exactly how it happened, that he ended up at Duke Zeibert's restaurant. There was a camera crew going around town, getting thoughts about Martin Luther King Day, and they see Jimmy "The Greek." So they go over and ask him about Martin Luther King Day, and one thing leads to another. All because the freaking camera broke!"

"I remember talking to Jimmy in my hotel room that night. There were literally reporters walking around the hotel looking for him. The whole scene was beyond belief. I remember talking to Brent about it, and he was very undone. Irv was a bit more level-headed about it, but he knew it was going to be really bad for Jimmy."

On the show the next day, Brent made the announcement live on the air that Jimmy had been fired. It was just a bizarre day on set. The opening credits of the show were omitted during the theme song when the broadcast came on the air. It was too late to edit out Jimmy's name while keeping everyone else, so the producers had to skip the opening credits.

I still almost expected to see Jimmy show up at any point, with that loud distinctive voice of his. We were on location in Washington DC to cover a playoff game, but instead of the football game being the focus, the controversy surrounding Jimmy and his comments made far bigger news. Regardless of how anybody at CBS felt about Jimmy, nobody wanted to see him go out like that. Brent reflected that in his comments, after Pat Summerall and John Madden opened the show in the booth, then kicked it to Brent.

"You know, on Friday afternoon here in Washington, our former colleague Jimmy 'The Greek' made some regrettable and offensive remarks for which he has apologized," said Brent, standing down on the field along the sidelines. "Yesterday, CBS issued a statement disassociating itself from those remarks. It goes without saying that his comments do not reflect in any way the thinking or attitudes of the rest of us here at CBS Sports. While we deplore the incident this weekend, we are saddened that our twelve-year association with Jimmy had to end this way. And the *NFL Today* will continue live from RFK Stadium in Washington in just a moment."

I remember Brent and I discussing how the show would be different without Jimmy, and we wondered if Jimmy could withstand the fallout.

"It was stupid for Jimmy to say any part of what he said, but I don't think he was trying to be malicious," Musberger said. "He was actually trying to show off with the camera on. People have asked me plenty of times how Irv and Jimmy got along. They were good friends. If the Greek was any kind of racist, he certainly hid it from the rest of us.

"I just thought it was stupid, and he was talking about a subject that, without a shadow of a doubt, Greek was not an expert. He had no business going down that road, and he paid a huge price." The day after making the remarks, Jimmy knew his world was crumbling.

"Please leave me alone the rest of the day," Jimmy told United Press International. "I got enough headaches right now. I mean, I'm seventy years old and I've never been in trouble in my life over anything like this. I didn't think I said anything—please, please, I don't want to make it worse for CBS than it already is."

Rev. Jesse Jackson met with Jimmy as the controversy swirled, and used the situation to call attention to the NFL's woeful minority hiring record among their coaching staffs and front offices.

"Individuals who make statements that are insulting are dispensable and they go," Jackson told United Press International. "But the policies that remain must be changed."

Michael Wilbon, later of ESPN but a columnist with the *Washington Post* in 1988, skewered Jimmy for his remarks.

"The events of the last 24 hours make it all too difficult to accept 'The Greek's apology," Wilbon wrote. "I am black, and I am offended as much by his apology as his initial remarks.

"The shame is not only that 'The Greek' said what he and others like him have believed all their lives, but that he doesn't understand what he did wrong or how it could offend people."

Two days after his statements, Jimmy gave an interview to *ABC News* after meeting with Jackson, and "The Greek" looked beleaguered.

"I'm in trouble," Jimmy said in the interview. "I've been in trouble before but I've always worked out of it. This one is a little bit different, but with the reverend's help I'm sure I'll be alright."

The fact of it was that Jimmy was never really alright again. At the time he had an apartment in New York, I think he had an apartment in Las Vegas, and he had a house in Durham, North Carolina. A few weeks after this happened, I visited him down there. It was sad, and he was sad. Pretty soon, he had lost everything. He had a newspaper column he wrote. He lost that. He lost his contacts in football. His reputation as an oddsmaker was hurt badly because he was kicked off the air. And there was no way he was going to get another job in television.

"Jimmy was in the last year of his contract when he made those remarks, and I already thought he was losing some of his energy," Veras said. "He didn't want to go live. We had to re-tape him a lot. I think part of the reason he did what he did was to let us know he was going to be bombastic. But he went too far because I think he saw and felt things slipping away. His demise coincided with the emergence of ESPN. They became major players in the NFL in 1986 when they got NFL games, and then they were doing a one-hour pregame show. They were bringing fresh blood to the set like Chris Berman, like Tom Jackson, and they were a new, major competitor.

"In his early days on the show, Jimmy was giving good league information and was close to a lot of owners. But he wasn't getting that anymore. That was sort of passing him by. We brought in Will McDonough. Phyllis left. The transition was happening."

After the incident, I would call him a couple of times a month just to see how he was doing. Every time I talked to him after that, his health wasn't good, and I think he sounded more depressed, a mental issue more than a physical issue.

It was sad. Jimmy's state of mind changed. He had always been kind of an upbeat guy. If you went to a restaurant, Greek would be the guy in the middle entertaining everybody. Some of the stories were real, some of them weren't, but everybody was having a great time. That's what he liked, being the center of attention, being the social guy.

When I'd call him, he'd say, "Irv, you're the only one from CBS who stayed in touch." At some point, he wrote me this letter, which I have kept for more than thirty years. It reads like someone else probably helped him write it, maybe an attorney or something. When you see his comments at the bottom, you can tell it's a totally different kind of writing style, compared to the letter.

Dear Irv:

I regret that I have to write this letter, but it is necessary.

Recently I made some remarks on television that were offensive, not only to Black Americans but to all Americans. It was not my intention to offend anyone, but I did. As a result I embarrassed myself, my family, my friends, and my employer.

It would do no good to explain that I was actually trying to say something very positive about Black athletes—that they work hard, they are disciplined, they overcome great obstacles and odds to become great athletes, and they are highly motivated. (I said "hungry") in the interviews. No positive explanation, however, can overcome the negative remarks that were made and the offensive way they came out.

Thus, the only thing I know how to do as a human being is to say I am sorry, offer my regrets, and ask for forgiveness. In all honesty, more than the loss of my job at CBS, the thing that hurts me most is the loss of your respect for me. The job I can do without. I need my self-respect back. The only way I know to do that is to ask for forgiveness from the people I have offended—Americans generally, Black Americans in particular, and Black athletes especially. That's why I am writing you—to ask your forgiveness.

Sincerely,
Jimmy

P.S. How do you fite (sic) this?

That last line is typical Jimmy, along with the misspelled word. Jimmy was a street guy. He was an old-fashioned gambler. If he shook your hand on something, he'd stake his life on it. That's what hurt him more than anything else with CBS. He had a contract. He knew all those people. They were supposed to be his friends. All of a sudden, they were gone. All of a sudden, he went straight to the floor, all the way down. He said I was the only one from CBS who called him regularly, who stayed in touch with him afterward.

With him, a handshake was better than a signed contract. That's what he couldn't understand. When the pressure was on, where were all his friends? They disappeared.

"To this day, I feel badly about the way the Greek bowed out and never got another chance," Musberger said. "He passed away a very sad character. That's about the only controversy I've been involved in that really bothers me."

I think even the executives felt badly about what happened to Greek, but he became a figure that nobody in television would touch.

"The Greek was a full-blown, 100 percent American character," said former *NFL Today* executive producer Ted Shaker.

"He was a completely unique individual. And there was good and bad in that.

"For the most part I think he was a good person. He was a generous person. But he was also wacky. The least wacky person on that panel was Irv Cross. Everybody liked Irv. Everybody respected Irv and treated him with that kind of special respect. It's not surprising to me that Jimmy would feel comfortable with Irv, because you could talk to Irv. If you told Irv something personal, it wasn't going anywhere. He was a quality guy."

Greek's demise was another lesson in life. You have to be careful what you say, and how you say it. If it's on the air, you can be here today, gone tomorrow. It's even more true now. For every person on the air, there's thousands sitting there ready to take your job. They'll never have a problem finding somebody else. You aren't that good. They can do without you, and this thing will just keep rolling.

And with "The Greek," there were other issues. The league was not always happy with his presence on our show.

Pete Rozelle (NFL commissioner from 1960–89) and others were trying to distance themselves from the gambling community. You've got the country's top oddsmaker on CBS talking about football every week. What kind of a contradiction is that for crying out loud? I know the league was always a little nervous about "The Greek." It might have been a way for CBS to let him go. CBS and the NFL have been partners forever. They might as well be working out of the same offices. If the choice was to keep Jimmy on the air, or responding to a call from the league office to "get rid of that guy," you know how that was going to play out.

BEARING THE CROSS

When Jimmy died (April 21, 1996), I think he died of a broken heart.

16

ME AND BRENT

THE *NFL Today* gave Brent Musberger the perfect platform to display his talents to the country every Sunday. I still get chills whenever I hear that signature catchphrase Brent used to open the show: "You are looking live!" It's like an alarm clock goes off in my head, the camera is on me again, and I'm hearing that familiar opening theme song.

The live element of the *NFL Today* was a huge part of what made it special. People knew they were "looking live" when we opened the show, and they saw that live shot. If the weather was bad in Chicago, or Green Bay, or Minnesota, you knew it. You could see it. And you can bet that live visual was important to fans, especially those who had monetary interests in the upcoming games.

Brent had such a smooth way of weaving up-to-the-minute information into his segments without breaking his rhythm—or our rhythm. You had to listen to Brent carefully to keep up with him, because he was fast and would adlib if he thought it would make the segment better. But I trusted him to lead us in the right direction. He was the quarterback. When he called an audible, I picked up on it, and went with it.

"Brent Musberger is probably the finest sports studio anchor who has ever done the job," said Ted Shaker. "I'm not saying that Bob Costas or Bryant Gumbel or Greg Gumbel aren't great as well. But I do believe that Brent was such a master at juggling all these balls.

"We would do three different pregame shows every Sunday for different regions of the country. Then we would do multiple halftimes. If there were seven or eight games on a Sunday afternoon, we would try to service each one of them with a unique halftime. It was like election night every Sunday afternoon.

"Wussler needed someone who was a master at keeping things running. We would mess up, and Brent would cover it over. He might turn to Irv to ask a question while we were getting our act together in the control room. It was a fire drill. It was unique for that time, and Brent was the catalyst for making it work."

Fate has a funny way of bringing people together, and it was that way for me and Brent. We both went to Northwestern together at the same time, but I didn't meet him until I was working for CBS, never thinking we'd end up spending so much time together on a show that was so successful.

"Irv doesn't remember meeting me at Northwestern, but I remember meeting him," said Musberger. "Guys on the football team had jobs. I was living in one of the dormitories. Irv's job was to make sure the washrooms were in good shape, and if they weren't, he was supposed to tell the janitors about it. I was actually brushing my teeth one day when he came in.

"I knew who he was immediately. He didn't know who I was from Adam. But I knew who he was, because I was following all of Northwestern's teams very closely, writing for the *Daily Northwestern*. I was around the football team a lot. I was one of the guys that the newspaper depended on to get quotes from [head coach] Ara Parseghian.

"I had no idea that some of the upperclassmen writers at the paper who had already dealt with Parseghian were intimidated by him, so they would send me to get quotes from him. Ara would look at me with those piercing eyes he had, stare me down a little bit. Ara told me that Irv was one of the best all-around athletes he ever had. He was a two-way player on the football team, and a track guy.

"Irv was nice to me the few times I talked to him. I'm sure I told him my name, and I'm sure he couldn't remember that moment now to save his life. But I never forgot.

"Fast forward to 1975 when we were putting the *NFL Today* together. The *NFL Today* was Bob Wussler's brainchild, and when he asked me if I knew a guy from Northwestern named Irv Cross I said, "He may not remember me, but I remember him as an extremely polite young man, and a great athlete.

"The *NFL Today* was demanding, but I absolutely loved doing it, and Irv was part of the reason. It was comforting to have someone like him alongside, because if there was a highlight I was uncertain about, or if there was a player I wasn't sure about, I could turn quickly to Irv and he'd pick it up. That was security for me when I had to do all the highlights. God bless Irv, because even if the other two on the set were upset with me, Irv never was."

If you spent one day working with Brent, you would come away knowing that he was a perfectionist who always wanted to get things right. He was totally prepared for every show. I took pride in being that way myself. Maybe that's why we clicked.

I always felt Brent respected the information I brought to the show. He knew I had solid relationships with coaches and players. He knew I could recognize some strategic things that happened during games which neither Jimmy nor Phyllis could. I had been on the field. My knowledge of the game was where I could bring more strength to the show.

So when situations like that came up, Brent would throw it to me with something like, "Irv, what did you think about that play call in the final two minutes?" Then I could pop in with my opinion after he had given me a terrific setup.

"I really believe that the only reason the *NFL Today* worked so well, for so long, was that Irv Cross was such a gentleman," Musberger said. "When we added Jimmy 'The Greek,' we had more egos in that room than any broadcaster should ever be asked to handle. The only person who kept the ship running smoothly was Irv. He never asked for extra minutes. He never asked for extra stories. He was just a really good guy and, among the four of us, he was by far the most knowledgeable football person. Not only did he play, he had been around coaching staffs. Sometimes after the games had ended on Sunday, the rest of us would start blabbing about one thing or another before we took off. Irv would still be on the set, quietly watching film. He was involved in the product of football.

"It's like a football team, when you have an offensive lineman who does a great job and nobody recognizes him because the quarterbacks and the running backs get all the publicity. Irv Cross was like our entire offensive line. Of all the people I've worked with in broadcasting, and that includes a lot, one of the kindest and nicest individuals of all time is Irv Cross.

"Even today, every other month or so, somebody will ask me, "Whatever became of Irv Cross?" You see the smile on their face when they ask. You can tell Irv was someone who made them feel good. That's the kind of warmth he projected, and it was consistent.

"Did I ever see Irv lose his temper, in all the years I worked with him? No. If he did, it would've only been for a few seconds, and then when I looked over at him, he'd probably be smiling again. He was such a gentleman. I'm sure he could tell you about moments when he felt slighted, or when he felt he was being overshadowed by Phyllis. But he never portrayed it. That's just not how he dealt with people.

"I'm sure that helped him in other jobs he had. It's a great skill, man. And not everybody has it. In this business, there are egos on top of egos, but not Irv. He's the best."

17

ME AND JAYNE

JAYNE Kennedy is a beautiful woman, as beautiful on the inside as she is on the outside. She has the kind of personality you connected with immediately. When Phyllis married former Kentucky governor John Y. Brown, started a family, and left the *NFL Today* for the first time in 1978, that meant one of the most coveted jobs in television was now available.

Now it was 1978, the NFL had far more black players, and I hoped I had opened some doors for blacks in television with our show's success. But would CBS really put two black people on the same show?

In a *People* magazine article, then-CBS associate director of talent Linda Sutter said, "I'd be lying if I didn't admit there was a lot of conversation about two blacks on the show."

Jayne also knew that having two black personalities on the show might give CBS pause.

"Just getting the job was a real struggle. For African Americans in the seventies, Hollywood was a very small community. You pretty much knew everybody. Whether it was Jim Brown or Fred Williamson or Sugar Ray Leonard, all of them were basically my friends.

"The opportunity came to audition for the *NFL Today* and they were looking for a woman. I was represented by International Creative Management at the time. They didn't want to submit my name, because, they said CBS was looking for 'journalists.'

"But I said, 'I can do this job. I know sports, I know football.'

"That didn't seem to matter at first. I wasn't sure I was going to get the job.

"Even after some other women interviewed and were turned down, they still refused to pursue the opportunity for me. I called Jim Brown, he talked to Bob Stenner, who was the game producer for CBS Sports. I finally got an audition.

"After I did the audition, Brent said, 'I want Jayne. We don't even need to interview anybody else.' The producer and the director both wanted me, too.

"But, they still wouldn't hire me until they sent my tapes to those Southern affiliates. You see, they already had their one black person in Irv. I was going to add more black to the mix. The solution was to put Jimmy 'The Greek' out front on the desk more often, so there wouldn't be two blacks and one white out front. Then I got the job."

I can't imagine how difficult it must have been for Jayne to land that job. Who wouldn't want to join the No. 1 NFL pregame show? We were being challenged in the mid-eighties by NBC's pregame show, but they had not supplanted our position as the clear No. 1 pregame choice with viewers. And my bosses were brimming with confidence.

"You can slice it any way you want—we're still cleaning their [NBC's] clock," Ted Shaker told the *Washington Post* in 1985. "Are we fat and lazy? I think we'll beat them on any story in the NFL. We worry about our level of quality. We're not concerned with NBC."

However, Phyllis's departure could have been hurtful to the show's popularity, considering her huge following. The competition to replace her was fierce, and I'm told more than seventy people auditioned to replace Phyllis.

Jayne was the winner, and it was a great choice.

"We didn't want the hardcore sportswoman, but a feminine combination of sports and entertainment," Sutter told the *Washington Post* after Jayne was hired. "On this show the female part is the entertainer. It's helpful if she knows sports. In terms of sports awareness, the female athlete is aggressive. What we wanted was a soft person, in the McLuhanesque sense, a soft person entertainer."

I'm glad my presence on the show didn't ruin Jayne's chance to get the job. By that I mean, the *NFL Today* already had one African American. When I broke into the NFL in 1961, there was definitely a quota system for black players. If you were black, and you weren't good enough to start, or to become a starter in the near future, you would probably get cut. Many teams also wanted to have an even number of black players, so they could be paired evenly as roommates on the road.

Thank goodness, CBS decided that two blacks wasn't one too many. I was a little concerned about the continued success of the show when Phyllis left, but in came Jayne and I immediately stopped worrying. From the moment I met her, I knew it would work. She didn't miss a beat.

"As stunningly beautiful as she was, her softness came through the camera," said Podolsky. "Wussler wanted her on the show because he knew she had a magnetic personality, and players would want to talk with her. And she understood sports."

Jayne grew up around sports, was very athletic, very smart and, as a former Miss Ohio, she knew about competition. Being around both Jayne and Phyllis, I learned something about how competitive those beauty pageants were. You had to be tough. You had to be confident. Jayne had all of that and more.

"We had auditions, and there were a lot of women who came in," Musberger said. "It was ridiculous how much better Jayne Kennedy was than any of them. Because she had great knowledge of athletics and football, it was not even close. It was the easiest vote I'd ever been involved with."

Talk about having a face for television! Aside from her vast knowledge, Jayne was stunningly beautiful. I had seen people, especially women anchors, take an hour or more in the makeup room getting ready for a show. Remember, this was live TV. If something didn't look right, the camera would magnify it.

Jayne didn't need an hour for makeup. She didn't need anything to enhance her beauty. I remember one Sunday she came to the set and didn't have much time to get ready for her shoot. Jayne sat down at the desk, took a makeup pad out of her purse, and dabbed her face a few times. Then she took a couple of swipes at her hair with her comb before she put her purse down.

"I'm ready," she told the camera guy.

The camera guy starts moving around, checking different angles before he stops and starts laughing.

"With her, I can't ever find a bad angle," he said.

I started laughing.

"Like they say, 'Black don't crack,'"

Then I started thinking to myself and laughed again. *I'm one of the luckiest guys in the world. I'm doing something I love, sitting next to Jayne Kennedy at work. How many guys out there want to trade places with me?*

The *NFL Today* continued in its No. 1 spot with Jayne replacing Phyllis and bringing strong stories to the show. But TV critics were hard on Jayne when she made a mistake—to me, harder than they had been on Phyllis. All I could do was support Jayne as much as possible.

"Irv was always himself, always a gentleman," Kennedy says of her days on *NFL Today*. "There were plenty of other people in the sports industry who were looking to stab someone in the back, just to get a foot up. But when you hear people talk about how nice Irv was, it's because he truly was.

"The Greek and I got along, but he was like a big old angry Teddy Bear. Brent and I got along fine, but Irv was the rock for me. I had never done live television before. Irv was the one person on that set who was always helping me. With everyone else, it was always sink or swim. But Irv was always the one who reached out and said, 'Let me know how I can help you.'

"It was probably one of the most difficult jobs I ever had. We were live. You didn't have the technology they had today, so you'd have maybe 17 or 18 monitors, people handing you stats under the desk, producer in one ear, director in another, and the four people on the desk trying not to talk over each other.

"We weren't scripted. It was a real challenge. Remember, some of our audience started at halftime of one game, then another audience would start at a different time. You're trying to remember what's fresh to this city, what's fresh to that city. Then I had to fly back to LA that night.

"I took a lot of criticism. One of the knocks on me was that I didn't know anything about sports. Not true. I grew up a sports fan in Cleveland. My father was a huge sports fan, and he had five girls before he finally had a son. So I grew up with sports. But when I came on the *NFL Today*, there were people in the media ready to criticize me from the start, and there were men out there who loved football that didn't want women to have anything to do with it. You'd hear about that. I had some tough articles written about me, some that were really unfair. It seemed like every day there was somebody trying to knock me down.

However, Jayne's stay on the *NFL Today* only lasted two years, before Phyllis returned in 1980.

"CBS fired me two years later," Jayne said. "They told me it was impossible to be fully committed to the *NFL Today* desk, because I had also taken a job to work as an actress on an NBC series.[1] However, as Brent was also working as an anchor in Los Angeles during the week, I thought it was a double standard that he could do that but I couldn't.

"They didn't tell me I was being fired right away, even after they had already decided to bring Phyllis back. When

I found out, I was in a helicopter doing a pre-game report at the Super Bowl in Pasadena. So when I got off the helicopter, I was so angry, I started running toward the booth. Irv was the first person I saw. He just grabbed me and said, 'Jayne, there's nothing you can do right now. Just take a deep breath.' I'm glad he did.

"Irv was always in my corner. I have to be honest with you. I look at tapes of some of those *NFL Today* shows and the graphics and scoreboards look so outdated. I'm thinking, 'Wouldn't it have been nice to have all the technical stuff they have now back in the day?' But I loved the reporting. We won Emmys and it was an amazing show, one of a kind, the No. 1 sports show.

"We still have a long way to go in the way we treat women in the business. But when I look back, I smile when I talk about it. And one of my best memories is thinking of Irv. I really appreciated him. He was always a standup brother."

18

GOODBYE TO THE *NFL TODAY*

MY run on the *NFL Today* show finally ended in 1990, when the network decided to replace Brent and myself on the show with Greg Gumbel and Terry Bradshaw.

Brent's departure came first. During the Final Four weekend of 1990, word leaked that Brent was leaving CBS. It was huge news that made national headlines, and I didn't see it coming. Brent didn't seem unhappy at CBS, and the *NFL Today* was still king of the Sunday pregame shows.

However, much more was going on behind the scenes that I was unaware of. That's the way it works in network television. What you see in front of the camera is important, but what you don't see behind the camera is sometimes more important.

During my final year of working with Brent in 1989, he remained the consummate professional. He was always prepared, ever enthusiastic in front of the camera. However, Brent's contract with CBS was set to expire later in 1990, and negotiations had become testy.

The climax was on April 1, 1990, when CBS announced Brent was being fired. At first, some people thought it was an April Fool's Day joke. It wasn't, and nobody at CBS was laughing.

"It's not a joke," Neal Pilson, then-president of CBS Sports, told the Associated Press concerning Brent's ouster. "It's a difficult decision. It's never easy to deal with individuals with whom you have personal or business relationships."

After broadcasting the 1990 NCAA National Championship between UNLV and Duke, which the Running Rebels won by 30 points, Brent signed off to viewers this way, standing next to analyst Billy Packer.

> "As you know, this was my last assignment for CBS. After twenty-two years with the television network, radio network, and the stations, I have had the honor to work with some of the greatest directors, producers, and technicians in the world, not to mention my good friend Billy Packer. Billy, we have shared some great memories.
>
> "Folks, I've had the best seat in the house. Thanks for sharing it. I'll see you down the road."

A few days later, Brent wasn't as conciliatory when he gave an interview to Sam Donaldson of ABC.

"They conspired to get me out of CBS," Brent told Donaldson. Brent blamed his departure on Pilson and Shaker.

"These two men decided I was too big for my britches, and that they were going to take me down a peg or two, that I was uncontrollable."

It was an unexpected turn of events, and I wasn't naïve. I knew that Brent leaving would have huge implications for me and for the *NFL Today*. Phyllis had already left the show for good. The Greek was still disgraced in the business, unable to convince anyone to hire him.

With Brent, Phyllis, and Greek all gone, the only person remaining from the show's heyday was me. The chemistry that Brent and I shared no longer mattered. The *NFL Today* would need a different rhythm, and I knew that the musical chairs could leave me without a seat.

Not long after Brent left CBS, I got the news from Shaker that he was pulling me off the show. I wasn't surprised. I wasn't being fired from the network. I would instead be reassigned as a game analyst.

I accepted the decision for what it was—a change in direction. I was still under contract, and still enjoyed working at CBS. Shaker assured me that nobody at the network had any complaints about the quality of my work.

"Irv and I had a couple of conversations about where the show was going, and we may not have agreed, but it was always respectful between us," said Shaker when interviewed for *Bearing the Cross*. "Everybody knows about Jimmy punching Brent Musberger in a bar. We had situations where Phyllis or Jimmy would go nuts about not getting enough airtime. Those are things you expect in a long-running program.

"But Irv was always the consummate team player. He always represented CBS in a first-class way. That's who he is. When others were banging around, unhappy about this or that, he would always keep going, keep going, keep going. That contributed his longevity."

Asked about my departure from the *NFL Today* in a *Washington Post* article, producer Eric Mann said, "The decision was that with Brent being gone, it was a good time for a new start, a new approach."

The *NFL Today* would have a different foursome—Gumbel, Bradshaw, Lesley Visser, and Pat O'Brien. Even the look of the studio set was revamped—a further indication that the show was embarking on a new era, as was television in general.

I didn't watch much of the new *NFL Today* show and, as I found out, neither did Brent.

"It was extremely difficult for me to leave that show," Musberger said when interviewed for *Bearing the Cross* in March 2017. "The opening week of that next NFL season, I could not even bring myself to watch it. I was out in Montana at our ranch out there. I knew when it was on. I actually went for a long walk out in the hills instead of watching the show. It took me, I'd say, six or seven weeks before I could watch any of the NFC action on CBS.

"Was I feeling sorry for myself? Probably not. I had a good job with ABC. But I missed the live fire on the *NFL Today*. There was no doubt about that."

Brent has told people that CBS didn't want him to return.

"Neal Pilson has always been elusive about why he called off negotiations with my brother [and agent] Todd [Musberger]. I know privately Neal Pilson has told some friends of his, who happen to be acquaintances of ours, that he blamed Todd for the negotiations breaking down. Todd and I both believe that's ridiculous.

"Whatever his reason was, to the best of my knowledge, he never told anyone. I have no clue. And by now, so much time has passed, I don't think about it. People ask me about it, and when they do, that's the only time I think about it."

Neil Pilson remembers things a different way.

"We were unable to renegotiate our deal with Brent. We wanted him to work baseball starting in 1990, but his agent-brother and CBS got into a contentious negotiation. Frankly, we got to the point where we felt like we had people like Greg Gumbel, Jim Nantz, and James Brown, who were ready to take on the various roles that Brent was covering for us. So we advised Todd Musberger (Brent's agent) that we were not going to renew Brent's contract. It was the biggest story in sports for quite some time.

"Frankly when Brent left, it gave Jim Nantz and Greg Gumbel and James Brown real opportunities that they would not have gotten had we continued with Brent in the multiple roles that he was providing for us. So we made a difficult decision and it was a huge uproar, but I think CBS Sports is stronger for having made that call. All three of those guys, Nantz, Gumbel, and Brown, have had long runs with the network."

* * *

When the *NFL Today* began, neither ESPN nor FOX existed. Imagine that. It was a different time in television, with CBS and NBC holding a monopoly on NFL viewers. Not only that, but CBS had the contract to broadcast NFC games, which gave us all the bigger markets—New York, Los Angeles, Chicago, Philadelphia.[1]

The *NFL Today* dominated the pregame landscape in the seventies and eighties, but there wasn't nearly as much competition. Now NFL fans grab their remote and have a plethora of sports channels to choose from—CBS, FOX, NBC, ESPN, NFL Network, etc.

The *NFL Today* was getting a makeover and I wasn't part of the equation. Nobody in the NFL is indispensable or untouchable, and the same is true for those in television.

As much as I enjoyed being part of the *NFL Today* for so long, the schedule was demanding. I was rarely home during football season. We'd be on the air Sunday in New York, and I'd take the train back home to Philadelphia Sunday night. Monday was the one day I might be home the entire day. On Tuesday, if the Cowboys and Giants were playing the following Sunday, for instance, I'd be headed for a flight to Dallas to meet with coaches and players. Wednesday or Thursday night, I'd be headed to the Giants practices to meet with their people. At some point I'd have to look at the tapes, then put together the track and voice-over for the segment.

On Saturday we'd be in New York preparing for the show, and on Sunday, the next week's merry-go-round would start all over again. That's what it took to do the job the right way. But maybe it was time for a different routine. About the only criticism I read about my style was that I wasn't controversial enough, and TV was certainly starting to lean toward bigger personalities. I never focused on controversial stories because, frankly, I didn't want to.

"In the mid-seventies, it was very important for me to project a positive image," I told the *Washington Post* in 1992. "My role had an impact on a great many people. It's amazing how much influence you have being on television. I wanted to do things professionally, in a high-class, classy way.

"Yes, I sat on some stories, things that would involve a delicate personal problem, drug use, that kind of thing. I didn't think it was appropriate. I never felt very comfortable doing it. There were times in features you couldn't avoid it, but it was not something I enjoyed."

Maybe saying that out loud didn't help me land another job in television, but it was the truth. Players told me things in confidence that I never revealed, and I don't regret that to this day. I could have reported on some things that would have likely advanced my career, but reporting those stories would have violated some trusts. Becoming a larger figure in television wasn't worth becoming somebody that I didn't want to be.

"Being a nice guy, in Irv's case, I never saw as a handicap or problem," Pilson said. "Frankly, that's what we were selling.

"I'll give you an Irv Cross story you probably don't know. Back in the day, we used to have touch football games at the Super Bowl among the CBS staff and announcers. Irv was still probably the best athlete there. I would guess he was in his forties at that point. The game revolved around him, Johnny Morris, Tom Brookshier, and Hank Stram.

"The games got to be pretty intense because they were all competitive. I remember one time Brookshier came back to huddle grinning and said, 'Boy, I just knocked some guy right on his ass.'

"I had to tell him, 'Tommy, you just knocked over the president of the broadcast group. I would suggest you not do that again.'"

"Those were fun days, and Irv was a part of that for so long. Everyone missed him when he left."

In hindsight, once I was off the *NFL Today*, I probably should have pushed harder to secure a play-by-play job with one of the networks or with a team. But I had recently fired my agent and never hired another one. I thought my long-time association with CBS, coupled with my reputation, made it less critical for me to have an agent. If I really needed an agent later, I felt I could hire one later. But that probably wasn't a smart move. If you don't have an agent and you're dealing with the major networks, you're at a disadvantage.

If CBS felt it was time to make a change, I wasn't going to argue. I didn't think much about how the show would be remembered, but almost thirty years since Brent and I left, people still talk about the *NFL Today*.

"I think the *NFL Today* with Brent, Irv, Phyllis, and the Greek would give any of today's pregame shows a run for their money," said Stopak. "Frankly, there are a few dummies on the air today, in my opinion. Some are good, but some are very overrated.

"If Irv wasn't so good, it could've come off as CBS just wanting to have a token black guy. On the contrary, I don't think they used Irv enough. I think he and Brent had an especially good chemistry. That show broke a lot of ground, and they got loads of attention without obviously seeking it. But having Irv, I always thought, gave it more of a touch of class."

Even if I had been given the opportunity to remain on the *NFL Today*, I may not have enjoyed it as much with a different cast of characters. Clearly when I watch today's NFL pregame shows, there seems to be more emphasis on entertainment and less emphasis on providing information. When CBS decided to remove me from the *NFL Today*, there was talk that I had been on the show "too long."

"We went in a different direction," Rick Gentile, who was then senior vice-president of CBS Sports, told the *Washington Post* in 1992. "I guess there was a feeling that he wasn't contemporary with the players, that kind of thing. Twenty-one years [with CBS] is a long time. He had a great run. The business changes, the game changes, and you move on and do other things."

I thought that was pretty cold on Gentile's part, but television can be a cold business, just like football. At some point, you'll get a phone call or be summoned into a meeting that signals the end of the road. I didn't know Gentile very well, but he was basically telling me to turn in my playbook at CBS. I remembered some former teammates telling me what it felt like when "The Turk" knocks on your door at training camp. Well, the Turk at CBS had finally come to get me.

I have no hard feelings or bitterness. I knew they were just looking at the bottom line.

At the end of the day, I'm proud of what I accomplished during my time there. When I first came on the air, it was a big thing to have a guy on who could express himself and do well at that level. As I was able to do that, it opened the door for a lot of other guys. Today, nobody gives a second thought to black announcers, and I'm proud to have had something to do with that.

I did plenty of stories that I was extremely proud of while with the *NFL Today*. One of them focused on the lack of minority coaches in the league, which remained a relevant topic long after I was off the show. As somebody who once had aspirations to become a head coach, it pained me to see so many qualified black coaching candidates passed over for interviews during the seventies and eighties before the "Rooney Rule" was instituted in 2002.[2]

The final straw for me regarding the absence of black head coaches came when the Eagles considered David Shula to be their head coach in 1985, when he was only twenty-six years old. To choose a twenty-six-year-old at that point, no matter how qualified, would be a slap in the face to those who had put in decades of time as assistants. At the time, there were no black head coaches in the NFL, both Tony Dungy and Dennis Green were assistant coaches, and there were 32 NFL black assistant coaches at the time. Dungy had to wait eleven more years to get his shot as an NFL head coach in 1996 with the Tampa Bay Buccaneers. That's why the Rooney Rule has been important. Before that, too many black coaches weren't even getting a chance to make a case for themselves.

While I do not have many regrets during my run on the *NFL Today*, one that still sticks with me is that I did not have the chance to do more commentaries.

"I feel like they never gave Irv enough to do," Podolsky said. "The guys on ESPN today are known for giving their opinions. Irv didn't get much of a chance to give his opinion. Part of it was that Irv didn't really want to be controversial—but he certainly could have been used more. He wasn't just there to smile and look black. If anybody thought that, they were wrong. He was there to do a job, and he did it very well for a long time."

For me, trying to act like a Terry Bradshaw or a Deion Sanders on a pregame show wouldn't have worked. That's not my personality. While it was very clear that I loved working on the *NFL Today*, people looked for me to provide information and insight on football, not one-liners.

"The *NFL Today* was the originator of this idea of a wrap-around show around games," said Shaker, in an interview for *Bearing the Cross*. "When Bob Wussler created that program, he had the traffic cop with Brent, the analyst and ex-player with Irv, and a high-profile woman in Phyllis. It was diverse and different in its approach for its day. Then of course, Jimmy 'The Greek' provided the wink toward gamblers, pulling on his sources and inside information.

"It was unlike anything we had seen before. I joined in 1978 as associate producer. I came from CBS News, and I was very, very proud to be a part of the *NFL Today*.

"Irv Cross was a unique choice in my mind when Bob Wussler asked him to do the show. I'm not familiar with his thinking at the time, on why Bob chose Irv instead of Mr. X or Mr. Y. I wasn't there yet. But my sense is that Irv brought a certain level of elegance to the show. He's a very smart guy. He knew how to make his points well. His enthusiasm for the game was obvious. Whatever the question, whatever the situation that came up, Irv had the smartest football take on it.

"He also had a great sense of people. The players all had great respect for him, and found him to be someone they were comfortable with. God knows that isn't always the case when players are interviewed. He had a certain rapport that allowed him to move through the circle of players and coaches. They always seemed happy to see Irv, pleased that he was involved with the story.

"How well the chemistry worked among Brent, Irv, and Phyllis is the great mystery of it all. As for Irv, I think Bob intentionally wanted an African American to be on the show, and I think with Phyllis, he definitely wanted a woman to be on the show. He was trying to create a combination that would appeal to a broad audience. It was revolutionary at the time.

"Irv Cross is an absolute pioneer. You're talking about someone who was presenting himself in front of a major audience every week. The *NFL Today* had more people watching it back in the seventies and eighties than are watching prime-time television today. Everything today is so fragmented. When Irv was on the *NFL Today*, there would be nine to ten million people watching the program. It would be a top-10 show today in prime time.

"You had an African American, a beauty queen, and a gambler on a national TV show about football. Imagine if the show had not been as successful as it was. Had the show flopped, I don't think the decision-makers who followed Bob Wussler would've had the permission, or the balls, to try something like that anytime soon.

"I think Irv's success on that show is highly important. Irv is such a classy man, and he saw the big picture, and as the show grew in popularity, he never made missteps. He was as private a person as you can imagine, but affable, friendly, smart. But he didn't share much. I had no idea he was one of fifteen kids.

"Fifteen years is a hell of a long run. You put somebody on TV for fifteen years, and they usually wear out their welcome or blow themselves up. Changes were made, but Irv had an incredible run. That speaks volumes about his talent, ability, and how effective he was in that position. I have the greatest respect for him."

Even today, people sometimes do a double-take when they see me.

"Don't I know you?" they might ask. "You look familiar."

Most of them can't pinpoint why they recognize me. But if I mention the *NFL Today*, they start smiling,

"Irv Cross," they'll say. "I used to watch you guys all the time."

So did millions of others. It seems over the years, more people have gained greater appreciation for our work.

"Not so long ago, every Sunday football started at precisely 12:30 p.m., when Brent, Irv, Phyllis, and Jimmy would pop up on the screen for a 30-minute precursor to six magical hours of sports entertainment," wrote Angelo Cataldi in the book *The Great Philadelphia Sports Debate*, written with co-author Glen Macnow. "Back then, the hosts of the *NFL Today* on CBS didn't even need their last names. They were that popular."

It's rare to have a fifteen-year run on a show as successful as the *NFL Today*. For me, the years flew by. We did some great work together that has stood the test of time. I share a lifetime of memories with Brent, Phyllis, Jimmy, and Jayne, and with everyone who was involved with the show.

"There were a couple of groundbreaking things with that show that nobody talks about now because times have changed so much," Musberger said. "There were not a lot of young African Americans on television at the time. It was a step in our business that doesn't get a lot of notoriety, but Irv was the right person.

"Irv never called attention to himself, because that was just not the Irv Cross way. He was part of a different era.

Today, the athletes who call attention to themselves get the publicity. The media picks up on it.

"Irv was never interested in that. He really appreciated the game, how it was played, how it was coached, and the intricacies. He was not interested in Irv Cross's name being in the headlines. That wasn't on his agenda.

"I don't want to read his mind, but when you're one of fifteen children, you're part of a very large group. A single child gets a lot more attention and can become a little spoiled in the process. I say this about Irv, and I say this about Phyllis. Both of them deserve more attention than they ever received for their roles as pioneers.

"I got known because I just hung in the business, and I kept going, and kept doing it, and kept grinding it out. The Greek flamed out, so he became well known. The Greek was the total opposite of Irv. Greek never met a newspaper man or a headline writer that he wouldn't hang out with. It's not that one's right or one's wrong, it's just the difference in personalities.

"But Irv is an overlooked person on the *NFL Today*. He gave us credibility with the athletes. The racial makeup of the league was changing, but Irv broke through on the media side. He played a significant role in sports TV history."

I left CBS for good in 1993, after my contract expired. Truthfully, I felt I had been there long enough. I had parted with my agent, CBS had lost the NFL contract, and FOX had already hired a full slate of football people. I sensed it was time for me to make a change.

I never participated in the cutthroat side of the television business, and when an intriguing opportunity outside of television presented itself, I took it. When my run on national television ended, I didn't leave with sorrow. I left with pride.

19

BECOMING AN ATHLETIC DIRECTOR

"**W**HERE in the heck is Pocatello, Idaho?"

That's the question I asked my wife Liz in 1996, when Idaho St. was looking for an athletic director. Since leaving CBS in 1993, I had been seeking a job that would reconnect me with sports.

Being athletic director at Idaho St. sounded like a job that combined two things I cared deeply about: sports and developing young people. So I applied, although I knew nothing about Pocatello or the university.

Idaho St.'s program was having issues both on and off the field. Too much losing. Too many athletes failing to graduate or getting in trouble.

It sounded like a challenge, but my life had been full of challenges. And the Idaho St. University search committee said it was looking for an athletic director who would emphasize education and build winning programs the right way.

I had a lot of ideas that I thought would be good for the university, and their search committee seemed receptive to those ideas when I was interviewed.

I wasn't scared away by Idaho St.'s problems, or by the miniscule African American population in Pocatello. According to *Sports Illustrated*, in an article about my hiring, there were only 356 black people in Pocatello, and the town's population was 53,903. Much of the black population was comprised of student-athletes. Often, it felt like there were only two middle-aged black men in Pocatello—me and the school's basketball coach, Herb Williams. If either Herb or I went to the grocery store at night, by the next morning everybody in town already knew about it.

The move to Idaho St. was another example of how supportive my wife Liz has always been. We had moved to a farm in Virginia about 50 miles from Washington DC, and we were happily raising our two adopted children—Matthew, who was seven years old at the time, and Sarah, who was five. Liz, who is white, always looks for the best in people. If she had any trepidation about moving to Pocatello, she never expressed it.

"My wife is the one who encouraged me to take the job," I told *Sports Illustrated*. "She said, 'You always dreamed of being in sports management—let's do it.' All my life I've been the only black in my classrooms or the first black to do this or that. I am concerned a little bit about how my kids will be accepted. But our kids have always had a different take on the world. We treat people fairly, and we expect to be treated fairly."

With Liz's blessing, I took the job because I thought I could make a difference in the lives of young people. I'd like to think I did, but there were obstacles I didn't foresee. A large percentage of the university population was Mormon, and the Mormon bishop had an awful lot to say about what went on at the school.

It wasn't long before I had my first run-in with the administration. One of my first tasks was to hire a new women's basketball coach. The first name that jumped out at me was Ardie McInelly. She had great credentials, had won everywhere she had been, and was very impressive when she came to interview. We had a search committee, so I wasn't the only person with input. When the search concluded, there was no doubt in my mind that Ardie was the best person for job, and she was thrilled to accept when I offered her the position.

Well, the bishop had another candidate who he wanted to see get the job. The bishop's candidate was a nice guy, he had played basketball, but he wasn't a coach. He probably could have done OK, but Ardie was a better candidate.

I kept thinking to myself, "Here I am, a minority athletic director, and this woman had great credentials. Idaho St. had never had a woman as their women's basketball coach. There was no way I wasn't going to give her a fair chance, and she earned the opportunity."

The day Ardie was hired, I got a call from the bishop.

"How could you hire her over him?" the bishop said, referring to the male candidate he wanted.

There's no doubt in my mind that hiring Ardie hurt my tenure at Idaho St. from the beginning. Suddenly, not everybody was so happy I had arrived on campus. I got plenty of negative feedback from the community before Ardie had ever coached a game, but hiring her turned out to be a great decision.

"I had been an assistant coach at the Division I level for nine years, and before that a high school coach for six years," said McInelly. "When he gave me an opportunity to interview, I thought it went well. First of all, I'm a huge football fan. I remembered watching him with Phyllis George on the *NFL Today*. I was excited to meet him when I came for the interview. I still remember shaking his hand, and he looked at me smiling and said, 'Yup, my hand feels like an old football, doesn't it?'

"After Irv left Idaho St., we won the Big Sky conference championship in 2001 for the first time ever. We were undefeated in conference play. I give Irv the credit for that success.

"From Idaho St., I went on to coach at the Air Force Academy. I remember Irv as being a wonderful, charismatic man. When he walks into a room with that smile, the way he communicates with people, it makes them feel comfortable. I wish he could have stayed longer at Idaho St., but I understand the business.

"Basically, I owe him my life as a coach at the Division I level. It's all because Irv Cross gave me a chance. They may have wanted someone else, but it turned out well.

"I never knew that Irv was one of fifteen kids in his family. Looking back on that, it kind of makes sense because Irv was very inclusive. It didn't matter if you were a coach, a player, a trainer, a student, or someone on the administrative staff. Irv wanted to connect with you. He wanted to make everyone feel important. Maybe that came partly from his upbringing, being around so many people."

Ardie did terrific things with the women's basketball team, but we had problems elsewhere. Overall, when I arrived at the school, the overall graduation rate for student athletes wasn't very good.

Then something that really disturbed me happened. A "friend" of the university who was connected with a radio station tried to bribe me. He said if I could close a broadcast deal between his station and the university, there would be something in it for me.

That made me so angry, I felt like punching him. I told him I'd never talk to him alone again. I was grabbing both ends of my desk, and that's the only thing that kept me from standing up and kicking his butt.

If I had done anything unethical in Idaho, somebody would've known about it in five minutes. What would make him think I'd do that?

The football program was also having problems, although I hired a coach who I thought was excellent in Tom Walsh. Tom was a standup guy, he was good at what he did, he cared about the students, and he'd tell you to take a hike if you tried to interfere with his program.

"You have to give Irv credit for his convictions," said Walsh, who was an assistant coach with the Oakland Raiders for twelve years before coming to Idaho St. "He actually believed it was possible to turn things around with the athletic department as a whole. But check out their record at Idaho St. before Irv arrived, and since he has left. They haven't been able to win consistently with anyone. Irv understood what it took to be successful. He was overqualified, in my opinion, to be at Idaho St.

"There were always a lot of battles there. Battles about the budget. Battles about funding. Irv thought he had the commitment of the university to make it successful. I figured there was no way they're bringing in Irv Cross to be the athletic director if they're not going to fully support him. Not when they understood his background as a player both in college and in the NFL, and as a broadcaster. I guess they thought they could make a splash with the hire, because of the prominence of his name. They've had some great people and coaches go through that school, but were handcuffed when there. We wanted to elevate the grade point averages of students, elevate the graduation rate, but we didn't get to stay long enough to see a lot of things we had in mind come to fruition."

I thought I could make a difference at Idaho St., and my family enjoyed living there. I loved working with young people. But in November of 1998, less than three years after I took the job, they decided to fire me after the academic year, and Tom was fired in the middle of the football season.

When they decided to fire me, I probably could've stayed another year or two, but only if I had fired Tom. I wasn't going to do that, have him take the hit for me.

Despite my troubles at Idaho St., I wasn't done with athletic administration. I got another chance when I became Macalester College's athletic director in 1999. Macalester is a small school in St. Paul, Minnesota, and Liz's family is from the area. She wanted to move back to Minnesota, I was fortunate to get the job, and I spent seven happy years there as their athletic director.

"When Irv was at Macalester, he certainly had relationships with the community," said Dave St. Peter, who became the Twins' president in 2002. "We had asked Irv to serve on the Minnesota Twins community fund board of directors, which he was gracious enough to do. Then he ultimately served as the chair of the Twins Community Fund, which is our 501C3 which was governed by a public board that Irv would ultimately chair. During his time in Minnesota, he has become very active from a community perspective on a host of things.

"Part of our community fund goes to a program called 'Fields for Kids.' We build baseball and softball fields, and matching grants are provided. We work with local communities, local school districts, local Little League programs to build or renovate fields across not just the state of Minnesota, but the Dakotas, northern Iowa, and western Wisconsin. The Twins Community Fund is fully focused on growing the game of baseball and softball. That includes ensuring that we're focusing on a diverse group of young people. Irv was certainly part of the growth of the Twins RBI program, reviving baseball in the inner city, which is very focused on providing free competitive baseball programs for over six thousand youths in 2016. We're really proud of that, and it's grown a lot thanks to people like Irv.

"Irv's a colorful personality. I think he's a relationship-driven individual. Smart, articulate, but he cares first and foremost about people. He cares about the communities in which he lives. He brought tremendous perspective as an athlete, as an educator, and as somebody who was invested in his community.

"My formative years I grew up watching him, and Brent Musberger, and Jimmy 'The Greek,' and the rest of them. I'm fifty years old, and anybody who's my age or older knows about how different times were in television back then. The *NFL Today* was pre-ESPN, pre-internet. Beyond the newspaper that was your only insight into whatever was the key matchup that week, into the personalities of the players. Those guys were truly bigger than life. It was simpler times, but because of that, those guys became even more legendary, I think more legendary than the people that are involved in the multitude of today's pregame shows."

Macalester gave me an opportunity to interact with students the way I always wanted to. My door was open. Students came and talked to me about their studies, their life, their goals. I got to know many of them on a personal level. It was rewarding in a manner that I had envisioned, and we did some positive things for the community.

I'm thankful for my time at Macalester, and Liz and I still live in the Minneapolis area, where we're enjoying spending plenty of time with our first grandchild! Just another example of God's plan working out in my life.

I'm still part of the community in the Twin Cities where my wife and I have spent many happy years. There has definitely been life for me after the *NFL Today*. And I'm happy to say, it's been a fulfilling life.

20

GLAD TO BE POOR NO MORE

EVEN when I was doing the NFL Today and the show was at its apex, I never put all my financial future in one basket.

When I joined the *NFL Today* in 1975, CBS was paying me more than $200,000 a year.

That's good money now. That was REALLY good money in 1975, especially for a black man.

Yet, I saw my salary at CBS as just one part of my income. I knew TV might not last forever, and I had no idea the show would take off the way it did. I figured my run at CBS would last about three years. Guess I was wrong. Boy am I glad!

I never wanted to end up broke. Maybe it was a fear that was instilled in me from growing up poor. I've never been the type of person to have just one source of income. I guess that goes back to my childhood as well, having multiple jobs, always looking for ways to help my family make ends meet.

I'm heartbroken when I hear so many stories about athletes going broke shortly after their careers end. Some of them are even broke *before* their careers end. This shouldn't be happening, but there are several reasons for it.

Personally, I think players are less mature now than they were in my day. That may sound like the grumpy old man complaining, but I believe it to be true. Saving money was a priority. Taking care of your family was a priority. Almost everybody had an offseason job. Living within your means was important.

I noticed players' attitudes began to change after I got out of the game. When I was working for CBS, one player I interviewed was unhappy about his contract. He told me, "Irv, $1 million is chump change."

"Chump change?" I said. "Go find another job where you can make $1 million to work for 16 weeks." He thought about it, but he couldn't give me an answer.

Most of today's players need help handling money, and when they don't get the right help, bad things happen.

I helped former world heavyweight champion Joe Frazier with his money for a couple of years. Joe wasn't a wild guy or anything, but some people close to him wanted him to do more with investments.

So I would go watch him work out, then talk to him about a few things and make some recommendations—especially when he had a big purse.

I started working with him near the time of his first fight against Muhammad Ali, often called "The Fight of the Century," which was held March 8, 1971, at Madison Square Garden. Frazier won a 15-round decision, knocking Ali down in the final round and handing him his first defeat.

The coolest perk I got for working with Joe was that I got a ticket to that fight! I've never been to another sporting event like that. There was so much raw emotion in the air. Muhammad was the controversial figure then, coming back, trying to get his title. He became one of the most beloved athletes in the world later in life, but it wasn't always that way.

Back in the sixties and seventies, a lot of people didn't like Ali. They didn't like the fact he had converted to Islam. They didn't like him because he had refused to serve in the Vietnam War. And they didn't like him because he was so outspoken.

But Ali never let public opinion change him, and he eventually became an American icon. These guys who talk trash today couldn't hold a candle to Ali in that department. When he was young, Ali had the quickest tongue of anybody I've ever been around.

I got to know Ali in the early seventies when he was living in both Philadelphia and New Jersey, and I had just retired from the Eagles. I was walking in downtown Philly around Broad and Chestnut, and Ali was standing on the corner shadowboxing people.

"I said, 'Champ, what are you doing?'" He recognized me and we started to talk. I asked who was managing his money. He said he was being managed by a man named Major Coxson, a guy who had plenty of money, but nobody ever seemed to be sure exactly how he was making it. Coxson ended up being murdered in his home, gangland style, in 1973. Just another example of how you must be careful who you associate with. I'm glad Muhammad wasn't around Coxson when he met his end.

When it comes to finances, I think all of today's players should be involved in a responsible investment program with somebody they can trust. In 1978, I began a company called Irv Cross Enterprises. Our basic service was to invest money for athletes and help them with financial planning. We also booked them offseason speaking engagements and endorsements.

Cross Enterprises was designed to help athletes reach financial freedom. We offered them guidance to make financial decisions by working with experts that I had built relationships with, people who I trusted. I hired a tax planning firm, and a stock market research firm to help us create financial portfolios.

Of course, we came from a different era. Back in my day, athletes seemed to be more careful with money. Maybe it's because we didn't make as much. As an NFL rookie in 1961, I made $10,000. The highest salary of my career was $36,000. Today's highest-paid quarterbacks make more than $36,000 by halftime of Week 1!

My introduction to the business world came early in my career with the Eagles. During the offseason, I held a variety of jobs. I was a personnel officer for Campbell Soup, a sales trainee for O'Connor Corporation, and a stockbroker for three different companies—Bache and Co., Donaldson Lufkin & Jenrette Securities Corp., and Alex Brown & Sons. I was also the first black vice president of Lufkin & Jenrette.

Athletes only have a short window of time during their career to capitalize on their visibility. Our goal was to help our clients make business connections while they were playing that would last a lifetime, while maximizing the income they were making as players.

I also wanted young players, particularly young black players, to feel more comfortable making financial decisions when they entered the NFL. People don't realize what a major culture shock it can be for a rookie. You arrive in a strange town, away from your family and friends. Unless you're a top pick, you have to produce right away on the field to keep a roster spot. Some of your teammates are ten years older than you with a wife and kids. They're not looking to hang out with you after practice.

Put a twenty-one-year-old in a situation like that. Then hand him more money than he's ever seen in his life. It can be a recipe for disaster. I've seen it. You've heard about it. I wanted to do something about it.

Cross Enterprises helped players find places to live, got them speech courses if they wanted to pursue speaking engagements, tried to get them thinking about things beyond football. You'd be surprised, but some coaches don't want their players thinking about anything but football, 24/7. You can't develop fully as a person that way. Cross Enterprises also worked with the NFL Players Association to provide our services to players who were interested.

Football must be your priority when you're in the NFL, but it doesn't have to be your entire life. And you had better start thinking about life after football, because your career can end on any play. That's how I thought, and that's why I wanted my degree from Northwestern more than I wanted a career in the NFL. I knew the NFL wouldn't last. Knowledge never gets old. If you know how to create income with your mind, not just with your body, it creates self-confidence. It creates independence.

Many of today's players don't grow up with that mindset. It's about the money, the fame, and the lifestyle, while the education gets pushed to the side. I can't knock any athlete for chasing a professional career to improve life financially for themselves and loved ones. But if you're not careful, instead of you using the game, the game uses you.

I closed Cross Enterprises in 1990 when I met my current wife, Liz. We fell in love and moved to Washington DC. I just had the feeling it was time to focus on that chapter of my life, with a new wife, starting out together fresh. One of the main reasons I got divorced from my first wife is that I was never home. It put a strain on our relationship, and I didn't want to repeat the same mistake.

However, doors kept opening for me after my career was over—not because I was a great player, but because of the education I had, the contacts I made, and the qualifications I had from my education, as well as by gaining work experience during the offseason.

You're not going to be making one million dollars a year the rest of your life. When you career ends, that salary goes down to zero. If your whole career you were making one million dollars and you were spending five million, how would you think retirement would be an option? And once you lose your money, you can't go back and play four or five more years. That money's gone.

Here's my advice for today's NFL players: Pay yourself first. Don't worry about your teammate who just bought a brand new car. I never did. You don't need the fancy car, the big house. The second you can't catch that pass, complete that throw, make that tackle, or break that tackle, they get rid of you.

A lot of today's players leave school early for the NFL, then don't go back and get their degree. Now when it's time to get a real job, it's harder. These guys think, 'Hey, I played football at Whatever U.' So what. Can you sell anything? Can you write anything? Do you have any skill set that would make me want to hire you?

I'm approaching eighty years old and have some health problems . . . but thank goodness I don't have to worry about money! In fact, if I had a billion dollars, I'd use it to help other people, especially young people who needed the help going to college, or to make a better way for themselves.

I've been able to help my family, people I care about, and live a life I couldn't have imagined when I was growing up in Hammond. Even when I was doing the *NFL Today*, I'm glad I was thinking about tomorrow.

21

MY BIGGEST BLOOPER

THERE are moments when live television can go terribly wrong. I never cursed on live television, and I never made headlines by saying something insulting or incentive.

However, I had one moment when the cameras were rolling and I was caught in an embarrassing situation. Thanks to YouTube, plenty of you already know what I'm talking about. It happened on January 22, 1984, at Super Bowl XVIII between the Los Angeles Raiders and the Washington Redskins.

It was almost time to give my pre-game update on the sidelines. The director kept telling me, "Back up, back up." He wanted an angle where he could see me, along with the players getting loose. I wasn't on the field, but I was getting close to the field. Then it was time for my segment.

"The players love the field," I began, looking into the camera. "George Toma, of course, who maintains the field for the league office, maintains all eighteen Super Bowl surfaces, says this surface is by far the best surface for any Super Bowl game."

While I was saying this, somebody walked right in front of me and the camera while I was talking. Then somebody else nudged me from my right.

"We have a lot of people walking around down here," I said. But I kept going, still trying to get through my segment.

"But let me tell you, [Redskins kicker] Mark Moseley told me he had a dream Wednesday night, and he woke up in the middle of the night in a deep sweat, that he had kicked five field goals. He had to kick one field goal, a 45-yard field goal with just seconds left to go, to win the ballgame."

At that point, things really got bad. Mike Ornstein, who worked for the Raiders at the time, was screaming and approaching me from my right, telling me to get off the field. On live television! At the Super Bowl!

I admit, I was flustered. I started stammering into the microphone.

"Wait, wait, wait, wait, just, just, wait, wait, ah, ah, ah, wait, wait, ah, ah, ah, we're, we're on national television and I'll finish it right now," was what I blurted out. I turned to look at Ornstein, who was still screaming like a madman.

If you listen closely, you can hear Ornstein's response to me, which was, "I don't give a f***, I want you to move back."

But I still continued with my report.

"In any case, I asked Marcus Allen how he liked the field, he said it reminded him of the [Los Angeles] Coliseum and he feels right at home. Brent, I'm sorry, we have a lot of confusion down here. Go ahead."

The camera flipped back to Brent upstairs.

"I'm sorry too," said Brent, ever the professional. "Someone was trying to interfere with you down there, and he probably should have known better."

"It was really [former Raiders owner] Al Davis's fault more than anybody," Mike Orstein recalled when interviewed for *Bearing the Cross*. "That particular stadium, the old Tampa Stadium, had a really short sideline between the wall where the fans were and the bench. Our linebackers, Matt Millen, Rod Martin, Bob Nelson, and Ted Hendricks, were all lined up behind Matt while Irv was doing a standup.

"Matt didn't think they had enough room to get loose. So he yelled over to Al, 'What the f***? We need more room.'

"Then Al yelled at his henchman. That was me.

"'Get that f****** guy off the f****** field!' Al said.

"I really didn't see the camera, or the red light. I knew who Irv Cross was, because he was not only a nice man, but he was the biggest guy in the business at that point.

"But I always did what Al told me to do. I even taped my ankles before the game as a PR guy. That's how serious I was about whatever came my way.

"I did what I thought was the right thing at the time. Which was to tell Irv, 'Get the f*** off the field!'

"If you've seen the clip, you can see Irv start stuttering for a good 10 or 15 seconds. It had to be shocking to him to be interrupted like that, on live television. He was wearing his blue blazer, with the CBS logo on his chest. I probably didn't see that at the time. I was a crazy mother in those days.

"Then I looked up and I could see two guys running down the stands, coming straight at me. One was Val Pinchbeck, a longtime executive with the NFL, and the other was Joe Browne, who was the head of the league's public relations department. They had a bunch of other guys behind them. And they were all coming for me. I knew I must have done something pretty bad.

"Everybody was mad at me, except the players and Al Davis. They were good with it. So I just stood next to Al Davis for the rest of the game. Never left his side. Because nobody was going to dare say anything to him.

"The next day, after we won, we landed in California and were greeted by a big crowd. Of course a lot of cameras were on the players, but I also noticed a lot of cameras on me! Later on, I saw one of the LA newspapers had a story with the headline 'Even Irv Cross was sacked by the Raiders.'

"That moment has followed me for more than thirty years. You'll see some TV stations run that clip of me and Irv every year around Super Bowl time. It just got more famous and more famous with YouTube. It's probably my most famous moment in my forty-four years being involved in the National Football League.

"I really felt sorry for Irv, because for every two or three years, wherever he went, somebody would do stuff like sneak up behind him and say, 'Watch out!' He's such a good guy. He wasn't even mad at me that day. In fact, I've got a picture of him on my wall. We're standing at the LA Coliseum a year later, with both of us laughing.

"I've got nothing but respect for Irv. He was a black announcer in an era when we didn't have nearly as many black reporters. He was a unique figure in his time, good-looking son-of-a-gun, kept himself in great shape, looked like he could play at any time. And he always had a smile for everybody. Just a good dude.

"But when Al gave orders, I followed. It could have been Irv, Brent Musburger, or anybody else on the field at that time. It didn't matter. I just knew that we were in the Super Bowl, and our players yelled at Al, and Al yelled at me. So I had to get Irv.

"It just happened to be on national TV. It just happened to be with millions of people watching. It's amazing how many people remember that."

I figured Al Davis had put him up to it. He was standing about 20 feet away when it all happened.

Nobody at CBS got on my case about it. In fact, where was security?

Doing live television, you must laugh at yourself sometimes, because things will never go exactly as planned. That was one of those moments. It wasn't like I wasn't prepared. I couldn't have done anything to prevent it from happening.

I didn't see the clip until later. I cringed when I saw it, but at least I got through the segment!

22

WOULD I PLAY FOOTBALL AGAIN?
YOU BET!

WHEN I talk about the injuries I suffered playing football, people ask me if I have any regrets about playing. And to be completely honest, I don't.

Football requires a deep, personal commitment for it to be played the right way. The average person can't play the game at its highest level. There must be something different in the wiring of your personality. You must be willing to deal with the contact, to accept the physical challenge. It takes great courage. Not everybody has that. A special group of people play this game.

When it's fourth-and-goal at the one-yard line, there's going to be a heck of a collision. Everybody on the field knows it. You have time to think about that before the ball is snapped. Do you have the will to dominate the guy in front of you?

When Jim Brown was coming at you on a sweep, with John Wooten blocking in front of him, you had to sacrifice your body if you had a prayer to make the tackle. Trust me, I've been there.

There were times when Jim would get the ball on a sweep, and he would literally yell out loud, "Get 'em, Woot, get 'em." Jim was telling Wooten to wipe out the guy in front of him. I've been that guy. Getting trucked by John Wooten didn't feel good.

But this is what you signed up for when you played football. To see if you could make Wooten miss his block. To see if you could tackle the great Jim Brown in the open field. When you did it, you felt great. When you didn't, you felt defeated—but you picked yourself up and got ready for the next play. That's the essence of football. I loved it, and I believed that playing football helped build confidence in other walks of life.

Football brings out things you didn't know you had. When I watched the Patriots come back to beat the Falcons in Super Bowl LI, and Julian Edelman made that great catch late in the game, I jumped out of my chair. Amazing plays happen when people are pushing themselves to the limit.

I think too many fans look at a football game, almost forgetting that these guys are real people—husbands, fathers, sons, brothers. All during the week they're dealing with the same things we all worry about. But during those three hours on Sunday, all they're thinking about is the battle between the lines. It's an escape from everything else; an experience that's hard to describe unless you've been on the field, in the heat of the competition.

Football also forces teamwork. To be the best team, you have to play as a team. I don't care if you play offense or defense—it doesn't mean anything if you can't do things in concert with everyone else. Teamwork is more important than any individual person.

Several people I competed against during my NFL career stood out above the rest. One is an obvious choice—Jim Brown.

I looked forward to the challenge of playing against Jim. It always shocks me whenever I hear anyone speculate on how good Jim Brown would be if he played today. Do you realize who you're talking about? Saying Jim Brown couldn't play football today, at a superstar level, is like saying birds can't fly. He could probably play right now, and he's past eighty years old!

If you stopped Jim on one play, he'd usually come right back at you on the next play. He wanted to prove that he could run over you, or past you, just in case you thought differently. If you got Jim down low, while he was going East and West, you had a chance. He ran with his legs close together and you could trip him up sometimes if you went low. But if he started going North and South and built up a head of steam? Forget it. Not only was Jim bigger and stronger than most of the guys trying to tackle him, but he was also quicker. As big as he was, he was light on his feet, graceful. And he used his off-hand for leverage very well. It was hard to get both hands around him and wrap him up.

For some reason, Jim always called me "Herb." And for some reason, I never corrected him. Maybe because you didn't correct Jim Brown out of respect.

The first time I made the Pro Bowl in 1964, Jim was my roommate for the week in Los Angeles. Thing is, I rarely saw him. At night, he was out doing whatever Jim Brown was doing while I was in my room. But I've always thought he was a great guy, and I've admired how he always cared about other people. His intelligence was obvious, and you could tell his concern about people was genuine. Here he was, the best football player on the planet, and he could have been all about himself. But he wasn't. My respect for Jim has always been immense.

Another special opponent was Bob Hayes, the Cowboys great wide receiver. Unfortunately, Hayes had his NFL coming out party against me and the Eagles as a rookie, when he caught eight passes for 177 yards and two touchdowns. One of his touchdowns went for 49 yards, the other for 82 yards. I almost intercepted the second touchdown, but the ball glanced off my hands into Hayes's arms. The following footrace between myself and Hayes was no contest. I had never seen speed like that before.

I knew Bob would be great once he got more seasoning. I ran the 100 in 9.7 and he made me look like I was standing still.

With Hayes, you knew the Cowboys were going deep three or four times every game. Could you blame them? You already knew you couldn't catch him from behind. His speed was breathtaking. I remember another time playing against him in Dallas. I did pretty well in the first half. But in the second half they put three receivers on one side and flanked Hayes by himself on the right side. Don Meredith overthrew him on that play. But later in the game Meredith hit Hayes on a quick slant, he got the angle on me, and now I'm chasing him.

Suddenly, it occurred to me. *Irv, do you realize you're chasing the fastest man in the world? You're not going to catch him.* Needless to say, Hayes scored. I'm glad they finally inducted Bob into the Pro Football Hall of Fame. He wasn't just a great receiver. His speed changed the way the game was played.

When I was broadcasting, one player I always admired was Joe Montana. When he threw five touchdown passes against the

Broncos in Super Bowl XXIV, it was one of the greatest performances I had ever seen.

I'll never forget talking to Montana, in his room, a few days before that game. I had been covering the Broncos the week before, so I knew a lot about how they were planning to defend Montana. They were going to show him some defensive looks they hadn't used all season, hoping to confuse him.

As Montana talked to me in his hotel room, I started to think the Broncos had a decent chance. Montana was going to see some wrinkles from the Broncos that he never mentioned during our conversation.

But once the game started, it didn't matter. Montana had a beautiful mind when it came to football. When the Broncos showed coverages he didn't anticipate, Montana adjusted on the fly, like a chess Grandmaster who was always several moves ahead of his opponent.

Whenever Montana walked into the room for a CBS pre-game production meeting, all eyes were on him. He had that presence about him. What was impressive is that he wasn't loud and didn't make outrageous statements, but had that special something that made people gravitate toward him, and gave people confidence.

Brown, Hayes, and Montana all had skills that made them special, and football gave me the opportunity to see their greatness up close. Football helped instill within me the importance of teamwork. Football opened doors that would have never been open.

My concern is that injuries will eventually erode interest in the game. I used to work with Pop Warner football a few years ago, and I understood the concern many parents had about whether their kids should play. Making the game safer, and preventing catastrophic injuries, is something we need to be diligent about. I was a proponent of having more flag football leagues, especially for younger players. Their heads, necks, and shoulders simply weren't developed enough to handle some of the collisions.

We used to hear about it from mothers and fathers when their kids got hurt, even if they wanted them out there playing football. Once more and more parents start saying that they're not going to let their kids play football, and they go to soccer or basketball, or baseball, or something else, that's it. The law has been laid. It's not going to change. That's what the NFL should be fearful of right now.

There are a lot of parents right now trying to decide if their child is going to play football next year. Once they pull the plug, they're not coming back to football. And I don't see any way to remove serious injuries from the sport—not without drastically changing the game. It's a violent sport, a contact sport. To tell a parent that their child can play this sport for ten years and not get hurt is crazy. It's not going to happen. Linebackers are 250 pounds today. Some running backs are close to being that big, and they have speed!

But I don't have any regrets about playing myself. It might sound like the dumbest thing, but you go to a meeting with a bunch of retired guys and ask if we'd do it again, and we all say yes. We all wish we had played for more money—but we really didn't play for the money. My rookie year with the Eagles, my first paycheck was for $300. A preseason game netted you a check for $50. Your contract didn't start until the season began in September. We played because we loved the game.

So would I choose not to play football if I could turn back the clock? No way. It's part of what made me who I am. There's no doubt the NFL should do more for its retired players, particularly the older ones. But I'm not mad at the game. I'm grateful for it.

23

THE FOURTH QUARTER

I HAVE headaches 24 hours a day. Sometimes they're bad. Sometimes they're not-so-bad. But they never go away.

Due to the discomfort caused by those headaches, I avoid crowds. If I'm in a room with a bunch of people laughing, or joking, or watching TV, I'll leave because I can't take the noise. I get tired very easily. I can't even read a book for a few hours like I used to.

If I'm with Liz or somebody else I'm close to, I can have a great time. But when I'm around more than two people talking, it's hard for me to track the conversation. I feel lost. So I'd rather not be there. I just prefer to stay home, avoid lengthy conversations, and read my Bible.

It's no secret that a lot of former football players have neurological issues—the kind that cut you off from society. And when you're alone, you feel as though nobody really understands what you're going through. You start thinking dark thoughts.

I was saddened to hear that Gale Sayers, one of the NFL's greatest players and a contemporary of mine, had developed dementia. But I wasn't surprised.

The helmets guys played with during my era were inferior to what they have today. And the helmets we played with in high school offered even less protection, though the ones we had in college were of a better quality.

Sayers was such a great player that he was a target. Guys were going to hit him when he didn't have the ball. You can't just count his carries. He took more punishment than that. If Gale was hanging around someplace near a pile, close to some action, guys were going to try to hit him. He probably took a lot more blows than people realize, even though he was so elusive.

I'm going to have my brain tested for chronic traumatic encephalopathy (CTE) at Harvard after I die, but nobody will know for sure if I have it until they take an autopsy. As I've mentioned before, I suffered numerous concussions—particularly early in my career. But here's the big difference between my era and today. After suffering a lower-grade concussion, you'd be a little dizzy at first. But if you got some smelling salts, cleared your head, and went back into the game, you thought everything would be okay. With a more severe concussion, you figured you needed two or three days to clear your head, and then you'd be alright. You didn't think concussions would develop into a long-term problem after you retired.

Players from my era didn't realize that even after you felt OK, the brain bruise was still there. I remember sitting on the bench many a time when my head was foggy, hoping the offense would keep the football for a seven-minute drive so I'd have more time to recover. Because I knew once our defense went back onto the field, I was going to join them. Coming out of the game, or missing a series, was the last thing on my mind. If my head was clear enough to figure out which bench to run to, I was going to play.

When you reach your late seventies like I have, you're almost sure to have some health problems—whether you played NFL football or not. I consider myself to be lucky. I have a nurse who comes into the home two or three times a week to help me out.

I do believe the NFL is trying to help veteran players more than they used to, for public relations reasons if nothing else. But frankly, the best thing the NFL can do is to make sure we get the health care we need, and that our pension plan is sufficient to cover those expenses. To me, it seems our pension plan is upside down. The older you are, the more money you should get. Instead, the older players seem to get less, not more, than the younger players.

I don't drive a car anymore because I'm afraid I might not get back home. I lose track of where I am. If I get close to my house, I sense where I am. But if you took me to downtown Minneapolis, to a section I wasn't familiar with and said, "Irv, drive home," I'd never get there. All it takes is one building being torn down, or something changing on a familiar route, and I might as well be on Mars. My memory retention is not very good. And again, I consider myself to be lucky.

I know I repeat myself a lot when I talk. My doctor says I have mild cognitive dementia. My doctor tells me I have a 50/50 chance of progressing into more serious dementia. So there's a chance I'm going to be where Gale is eventually.

Thankfully I can cover it up pretty well. I'm still reasonably articulate, and if I wait between what you ask me and how I respond, I can have a conversation. I just pause a couple of seconds to digest what you said, then I respond.

The biggest cover-up I have is to keep talking, which forces the other person to listen. When our conversation has ended, you think I followed everything you said. I may have, but maybe I didn't.

Unfortunately, my health problems aren't just confined to my brain. I've got a sixth vertebrae problem in my back, and I remember exactly when that happened. I made a tackle playing for the Rams and my head was about waist-high as I headed for the ball carrier. However, one of the linemen blocked me and his facemask slammed into me between the bottom of my helmet and my shoulder pads and snapped my neck. Fortunately, it was a third-down play so I went off and had a chance to rest before the next series. But my neck has been kind of screwed up ever since. I played a couple of more years with my neck not being quite right, and that obviously didn't help. Meanwhile, I never insisted on anybody looking at my neck more thoroughly. I figured I had a little sprain or strain back there, and that it would be alright. But it has severely impacted the area between the bottom of my neck and the beginning of my spinal cord.

I've had some numbness in my legs because the nerve in my neck is pinched. Now I have a little balance problem. Sometimes I fall down. My balance is kind of screwed up, and my hands get numb. My legs from my knees down get numb. That's going to get progressively worse. The nerves just don't support the muscles anymore. Some nerves regenerate, some don't. I really don't have a muscle in my left arm anymore. My bicep is just flabby. I can pick up something that's about 20 pounds with my left arm, but if it weighs more than that I'm in trouble.

Through all of this, I know it could be worse. I can go through a long list of guys from my era with dementia issues—especially the linemen. Those guys lined up helmet-to-helmet with somebody every play, crunching each other's heads. So many great linemen I played with have already died—Lamar Lundy, Merlin Olsen, Deacon Jones.

Some of the rule changes the NFL has implemented have been helpful. Back in my day, the special teams unit was called the suicide squad. That was fitting. When you would cover kickoffs and punts, you were expected to run downfield as fast as you could to break the wedge. That's how some guys made their living as wedge-busters. That's almost insane, to run as fast as you can for 50 yards into a wall of humanity. But that's what guys did, until the league made some rule changes regarding the kicking game.

After a player goes down with an obvious head injury, I've heard some announcers say, "He'll get up. He's a tough guy."

What does being tough have to do with getting knocked out? His brain has just knocked against his skull, for crying out loud! How tough you are is irrelevant.

When I was working for CBS covering a training camp, I'd tell people if you were on the sideline during a game you'd never forget that experience. You feel the ground vibrate when the guys come toward you on a play. Then you hear those collisions, and the groans that follow.

I've spent plenty of time over the last fifteen years working as a member of the NFL Retired Players Association, trying to make life better for ex-players. But I feel like retired players of my generation are never going to get what they deserve.

The NFL has other priorities, like making money. Look at what has gone on the last few years, with franchises leaving cities. Those franchises that relocated were making money. But they wanted to make more money.

Owners today, and frankly a lot of today's players, don't have an appreciation of what people went through in the fifties, sixties, and seventies. Players were like raw hamburger being ground up. When you couldn't play, somebody else was brought in. That's why guys never left the field. They were afraid they'd never get back on. There were people dying to take their spot and the owners knew that. So the players were treated badly, and many of the players still alive are suffering.

We're a tool for entertainment. We bring the crowds. We do miraculous things. But nobody thinks about what it looks like in the training room when the game is over. Every single game, people are getting hurt. It's a contact sport, that's what people like to see, and when we call ourselves gladiators, that's the mindset we have.

But the damage being done is serious. The league is going to have to pay huge sums of money to players, but the NFL will find a way to slow those payments down. Guys in their forties and fifties who have Alzheimer's or another serous ailment will get the most money. Guys who suffer from something less serious will get less money, maybe not enough to get by.

Sometimes I think the league's position is to deny, deny, until enough of us die. As long as you can play, they're with you. But once the body starts to break, see you later.

The importance of protecting the health of football players is another subject that Brent and I agree on.

"The health of present and past players is the biggest problem that football faces today," said Musberger when interviewed for *Bearing the Cross*. "The NFL and the players are now aware of the situation. I'm not sure that back in the day, the NFL realized all of the long-term damage that was being done to athletes. They weren't as knowledgeable.

"Now, the reality of the situation is clear. I'd like to think today's players are in far better hands when it comes to identifying concussions and things that impact the brain. It's a multilayered story, a big story, and at the family level, it's a reason why the percentage of parents allowing their kids to play football is going down.

"The NFL has to address it. They can't hide from it. And you can't walk away from these players once they're done playing. From the time that Irv played until now, there's such an improvement in nutrition and weight training. How you take care of your body, how you work out. These guys are in far better physical condition than in Irv's day. But the negative of that is given the speed and the power they've developed, the collisions are more severe. To me it's football's biggest problem. Guys a lot smarter than me are working on it, and they must continue to do so."

As I've gotten older, close relationships have become even more important to me. There's no question that the relationships I built with teammates have become the biggest thing I've missed most about my time as an NFL player. Every guy who has been in the league any period of time has built a special relationship with somebody on the team, and probably somebody in the community. They become more like brothers than teammates. They become a part of your family.

That's one of the things you lose when you're out of the game. You don't build as many of those special bonds and relationships. I cannot talk to anybody else about some of the things that Maxie Baughan and I experienced. People wouldn't have any idea what we were talking about. But, every time we talk, it's like we pick up where we left off. We're joined at the hip for life.

I've reached the age where many of my friends have passed. When you lose your friends, you feel like you become isolated. Yet, I also realize I'm very lucky to still be here with my wonderful wife, children, and first grandchild.

I also realize that my time with the *NFL Today* show is probably the thing that most people will remember me for. The same is true for Brent, and Phyllis, and the Greek. I think all of us can be proud of our TV legacy with that show. I know from my conversations with Brent that he is.

"If we were all on the air today, we'd still be very successful," said Musberger. "There's not a doubt in my mind. First of all, we would've had more time. If that show had been an hour instead of 30 minutes, it would have been 100 percent better, because we would've had more time. Every person who worked on that show had a different role, but because we worked well together.

"If you look around at the landscape of pregame shows today, if I had to make any change, I'd say, you have to have a woman on the set, the way we had Phyllis. You also need a serious handicapper. I get what FOX does—they make fun of it and have comedians make certain picks. But they're overlooking the fact that millions and millions of NFL fans are participating in parlay cards, betting individual games, or are part of office pools. So they are very interested in winning and losing, and by how much.

"So if you put our group together today, we'd still be kicking ass and taking names. Irv would know as much about teams now as he did then. And people would still love him. Irv knew football inside and out, and that's always valuable commodity.

"He proved you don't have to have the big-name star player for a national TV show. For one year, the big name can work very well. But if the big name doesn't work as hard as Irv did, it's fluff. There's no substance there if he doesn't work like Irv did back in the day.

"It's true, the superstars will always get the first crack at it. But it was interesting that Bob Wussler did not move for a Hall of Fame player when he created that show. He went for somebody solid, somebody of quality, like Irv Cross. And man, did it work out great."

My life has worked out great as well. Both my father and grandfather lived long lives. Despite my ailments, I figure I've got a chance to get to a hundred years old or so!

When I got the call that I was receiving the Pete Rozelle Award in 2009 for longtime exceptional contributions to radio and television in professional football, I was caught completely off-guard. I thought the Hall of Fame committee was simply treating me to dinner in Canton. I said, "Why do you want me to come to Canton, again? We laughed after I finally understood I was receiving a prestigious honor. I knew no African American had ever won that award before. And I knew how much work had gone into my career, and into my life.

Then I thought about it some more, and I was moved by it. I remember what Jackie Robinson told me so long ago about making my parents proud. I met Jesse Owens once and always admired him. Those guys did things I can only dream about. I'm just grateful I was able to do things I never would have believed as a kid growing up in Hammond.

I've had plenty of time to reflect on everywhere I've been, all the things I've done, and all the impressions I may have left on people. I've concluded that you should do your job the best you can. You should live your life the best you know how. If you leave a mark that other people can see, maybe somebody will look at it and say, "I didn't know that guy did that. If he can do that, so can I."

Anything can happen in life, and a whole lot has happened in mine. I hope you enjoyed hearing about it. God bless you all.

CHAPTER NOTES

Chapter 7

1. As of 2016, it was listed as tied for the eighth-longest reception in school history.
2. There are currently seven rounds in the NFL Draft, with a total of 256 players picked.
3. Cross was drafted in the 15th round (117 overall) in the 1961 AFL Draft.

Chapter 17

1. The show in question was the short-lived *Speak Up America*.

Chapter 18

1. In 1993, the NFL accepted Fox's bid to televise the NFC on their network, starting for the 1994 season. It would be the first time that CBS would not broadcast football in thirty-eight years, and they would not air a game for four years, until 1998, when they acquired the televising rights for the AFC (taking those rights from NBC).
2. When I went off the air in 1990, there was one black head coach in the NFL (Art Shell with the Raiders). As of 2017, there are eight, which means that a quarter of all NFL coaches are African American.

ACKNOWLEDGMENTS

Irv

My wife, Liz, who encouraged me to share my life's story.

All my teammates and coaches who shared the pressure of competition.

Brooks House of Christian Service where I learned the most important principles of life:
   1. God
   2. Others
   3. Self

Clifton Brown, a writer blessed with the gift of putting my life into words.

My family . . . large and loving.

BEARING THE CROSS

Clifton

My wife Delores, for giving me her love and support, no matter the situation.

My daughter Ashley, who makes me proud and makes me smile every day.

My son Alex, who inspires me and believes in me, just as I always believe in him.

Irv Cross—a special person who trusted me to help tell his story.

Tim Smith, whose friendship led to this book becoming a reality.

Jason Katzman, an editor who became a friend during this process.

John Barry, who gave a young kid from Philly his first job in journalism.

Yeadon High School—a melting pot that prepared me for life.

And God, for showing me the right path, whenever I'm smart enough to ask for directions.

INDEX